TABLE OF CONTENTS

Top 20 Test Taking Tips

1. Carefully follow all the test registration procedures
2. Know the test directions, duration, topics, question types, how many questions
3. Setup a flexible study schedule at least 3-4 weeks before test day
4. Study during the time of day you are most alert, relaxed, and stress free
5. Maximize your learning style; visual learner use visual study aids, auditory learner use auditory study aids
6. Focus on your weakest knowledge base
7. Find a study partner to review with and help clarify questions
8. Practice, practice, practice
9. Get a good night's sleep; don't try to cram the night before the test
10. Eat a well-balanced meal
11. Know the exact physical location of the testing site; drive the route to the site prior to test day
12. Bring a set of ear plugs; the testing center could be noisy
13. Wear comfortable, loose fitting, layered clothing to the testing center; prepare for it to be either cold or hot during the test
14. Bring at least 2 current forms of ID to the testing center
15. Arrive to the test early; be prepared to wait and be patient
16. Eliminate the obviously wrong answer choices, then guess the first remaining choice
17. Pace yourself; don't rush, but keep working and move on if you get stuck
18. Maintain a positive attitude even if the test is going poorly
19. Keep your first answer unless you are positive it is wrong
20. Check your work, don't make a careless mistake

Quantitative

Numbers and Operations

Classifying Numbers

There are several different kinds of numbers. When you learn to count as a child, you typical start with *Natural Numbers*. These are sometimes called "counting numbers" and begin with 1, 2, 3 ... etc. *Whole Numbers* include all natural numbers as well as 0. *Integers* include all whole numbers as well as their associated negative values (...-2, -1, 0, 1, 2...). Fractions with an integer in the numerator and a non-zero integer in the denominator are called *Rational Numbers*. Numbers such as π, that are non-terminating and non-repeating and cannot be expressed as a fraction, are considered *Irrational Numbers*. Any number that contains the imaginary number i, where $i^2 = -1$ and $i = \sqrt{-1}$, is referred to as a *Complex Number*. All natural numbers, whole numbers, integers, rational numbers, and irrational numbers are *Real Numbers*; complex numbers are not real numbers.

Aside from the number 1, all natural numbers can either be classified as prime or composite. *Prime Numbers* are natural numbers greater than 1 whose only factors are 1 and itself. On the other hand, *Composite Numbers* are natural numbers greater than 1 that are not prime numbers. 1 is a special case in that it is neither a prime number nor composite number. According to the *Fundamental Theorem of Arithmetic*, every composite number can be uniquely written as the product of prime numbers.

Numbers are the basic building blocks of mathematics. Specific features of numbers are identified by the following terms:

Integers – The set of positive and negative numbers, including zero. Integers do not include fractions $\left(\frac{1}{3}\right)$, decimals (0.56), or mixed numbers $\left(7\frac{3}{4}\right)$.

Even number – Any integer that can be divided by 2 without leaving a remainder. For example: 2, 4, 6, 8, and so on.

Odd number – Any integer that cannot be divided evenly by 2. For example: 3, 5, 7, 9, and so on.

Decimal number – a number that uses a decimal point to show the part of the number that is less than one. Example: 1.234.

Decimal point – a symbol used to separate the ones place from the tenths place in decimals or dollars from cents in currency.

Decimal place – the position of a number to the right of the decimal point. In the decimal 0.123, the 1 is in the first place to the right of the decimal point, indicating tenths; the 2 is in the second place, indicating hundredths; and the 3 is in the third place, indicating thousandths.

The decimal, or base 10, system is a number system that uses ten different digits (0, 1, 2, 3, 4, 5, 6, 7, 8, 9). An example of a number system that uses something other than ten digits is the binary, or base 2, number system, used by computers, which uses only the numbers 0 and 1. It is thought that the decimal system originated because people had only their 10 fingers for counting.

➢ **Review Video: <u>Numbers and Their Classification</u>**
*Visit **mometrix.com/academy** and enter **Code: 461071***

Operations

There are four basic mathematical operations:
Addition increases the value of one quantity by the value of another quantity. Example: 2 + 4 = 6; 8 + 9 = 17. The result is called the sum. With addition, the order does not matter. 4 + 2 = 2 + 4.

Subtraction is the opposite operation to addition; it decreases the value of one quantity by the value of another quantity. Example: 6 − 4 = 2; 17 − 8 = 9. The result is called the difference. Note that with subtraction, the order does matter. 6 − 4 ≠ 4 − 6.

Multiplication can be thought of as repeated addition. One number tells how many times to add the other number to itself. Example: 3 × 2 (three times two) = 2 + 2 + 2 = 6. With multiplication, the order does not matter. 2 × 3 (or 3 + 3) = 3 × 2 (or 2 + 2 + 2).

Division is the opposite operation to multiplication; one number tells us how many parts to divide the other number into. Example: 20 ÷ 4 = 5; if 20 is split into 4 equal parts, each part is 5. With division, the order of the numbers does matter. 20 ÷ 4 ≠ 4 ÷ 20.

Parentheses

Parentheses are used to designate which operations should be done first when there are multiple operations. Example: 4 − (2 + 1) = 1; the parentheses tell us that we must add 2 and 1, and then subtract the sum from 4, rather than subtracting 2 from 4 and then adding 1 (this would give us an answer of 3).

Order of Operations

Order of Operations is a set of rules that dictates the order in which we must perform each operation in an expression so that we will evaluate it accurately. If we have an expression that includes multiple different operations, Order of Operations tells us which operations to do first. The most common mnemonic for Order of Operations is PEMDAS, or "Please Excuse My Dear Aunt Sally." PEMDAS stands for Parentheses, Exponents, Multiplication, Division, Addition, Subtraction. It is important to understand that multiplication and division have equal precedence, as do addition and subtraction, so those pairs of operations are simply worked from left to right in order.

Example: Evaluate the expression $5 + 20 \div 4 \times (2 + 3)^2 - 6$ using the correct order of operations.

P: Perform the operations inside the parentheses, $(2 + 3) = 5$.

E: Simplify the exponents, $(5)^2 = 25$.

The equation now looks like this: $5 + 20 \div 4 \times 25 - 6$.

MD: Perform multiplication and division from left to right, $20 \div 4 = 5$; then $5 \times 25 = 125$.

The equation now looks like this: $5 + 125 - 6$.

AS: Perform addition and subtraction from left to right, $5 + 125 = 130$; then $130 - 6 = 124$.

> ➤ **Review Video: Order of Operations**
> Visit **mometrix.com/academy** and enter **Code: 259675**

Roots and Square Roots

A root, such as a square root, is another way of writing a fractional exponent. Instead of using a superscript, roots use the radical symbol ($\sqrt{}$) to indicate the operation. A radical will have a number underneath the bar, and may sometimes have a number in the upper left: $\sqrt[n]{a}$, read as "the nth root of a." The relationship between radical notation and exponent notation can be described by this equation: $\sqrt[n]{a} = a^{1/n}$. The two special cases of $n = 2$ and $n = 3$ are called square roots and cube roots. If there is no number to the upper left, it is understood to be a square root ($n = 2$). Nearly all of the roots you encounter will be square roots. A square root is the same as a number raised to the one-half power. When we say that a is the square root of b ($a = \sqrt{b}$), we mean that a multiplied by itself equals b: ($a \times a = b$).

A perfect square is a number that has an integer for its square root. There are 10 perfect squares from 1 to 100: 1, 4, 9, 16, 25, 36, 49, 64, 81, 100 (the squares of integers 1 through 10).

Factors and Multiples

Factors are numbers that are multiplied together to obtain a product. For example, in the equation $2 \times 3 = 6$, the numbers 2 and 3 are factors. A prime number has only two factors (1 and itself), but other numbers can have many factors.

> ➤ **Review Video: Factors**
> Visit **mometrix.com/academy** and enter **Code: 920086**

A common factor is a number that divides exactly into two or more other numbers. For example, the factors of 12 are 1, 2, 3, 4, 6, and 12, while the factors of 15 are 1, 3, 5, and 15. The common factors of 12 and 15 are 1 and 3. A prime factor is also a prime number. Therefore, the prime factors of 12 are 2 and 3. For 15, the prime factors are 3 and 5.

The greatest common factor (GCF) is the largest number that is a factor of two or more numbers. For example, the factors of 15 are 1, 3, 5, and 15; the factors of 35 are 1, 5, 7, and 35. Therefore, the greatest common factor of 15 and 35 is 5.

The least common multiple (LCM) is the smallest number that is a multiple of two or more numbers. For example, the multiples of 3 include 3, 6, 9, 12, 15, etc.; the multiples of 5 include 5, 10, 15, 20, etc. Therefore, the least common multiple of 3 and 5 is 15.

➤ **Review Video: <u>Multiples</u>**
Visit *mometrix.com/academy* and enter *Code: 626738*

Fractions

A fraction is a number that is expressed as one integer written above another integer, with a dividing line between them $\left(\frac{x}{y}\right)$. It represents the quotient of the two numbers "x divided by y." It can also be thought of as x out of y equal parts.

The top number of a fraction is called the numerator, and it represents the number of parts under consideration. The 1 in $\frac{1}{4}$ means that 1 part out of the whole is being considered in the calculation. The bottom number of a fraction is called the denominator, and it represents the total number of equal parts. The 4 in $\frac{1}{4}$ means that the whole consists of 4 equal parts. A fraction cannot have a denominator of zero; this is referred to as "undefined."

Fractions can be manipulated by multiplying or dividing (but not adding or subtracting) both the numerator and denominator by the same number, without changing the value of the fraction. If you divide both numbers by a common factor, you are reducing or simplifying the fraction. Two fractions that have the same value, but are expressed differently are known as equivalent fractions. For example, $\frac{2}{10}, \frac{3}{15}, \frac{4}{20}$, and $\frac{5}{25}$ are all equivalent fractions. They can also all be reduced or simplified to $\frac{1}{5}$.

When two fractions are manipulated so that they have the same denominator, this is known as finding a common denominator. The number chosen to be that common denominator should be the least common multiple of the two original denominators. Example: $\frac{3}{4}$ and $\frac{5}{6}$; the least common multiple of 4 and 6 is 12. Manipulating to achieve the common denominator: $\frac{3}{4} = \frac{9}{12}; \frac{5}{6} = \frac{10}{12}$.

If two fractions have a common denominator, they can be added or subtracted simply by adding or subtracting the two numerators and retaining the same denominator. Example: $\frac{1}{2} + \frac{1}{4} = \frac{2}{4} + \frac{1}{4} = \frac{3}{4}$. If the two fractions do not already have the same denominator, one or both of them must be manipulated to achieve a common denominator before they can be added or subtracted.

Two fractions can be multiplied by multiplying the two numerators to find the new numerator and the two denominators to find the new denominator. Example: $\frac{1}{3} \times \frac{2}{3} = \frac{1 \times 2}{3 \times 3} = \frac{2}{9}$.

Two fractions can be divided flipping the numerator and denominator of the second fraction and then proceeding as though it were a multiplication. Example: $\frac{2}{3} \div \frac{3}{4} = \frac{2}{3} \times \frac{4}{3} = \frac{8}{9}$.

A fraction whose denominator is greater than its numerator is known as a proper fraction, while a fraction whose numerator is greater than its denominator is known as an improper fraction. Proper fractions have values less than one and improper fractions have values greater than one.

A mixed number is a number that contains both an integer and a fraction. Any improper fraction can be rewritten as a mixed number. Example: $\frac{8}{3} = \frac{6}{3} + \frac{2}{3} = 2 + \frac{2}{3} = 2\frac{2}{3}$. Similarly, any mixed number can be rewritten as an improper fraction. Example: $1\frac{3}{5} = 1 + \frac{3}{5} = \frac{5}{5} + \frac{3}{5} = \frac{8}{5}$.

A fraction that contains a fraction in the numerator, denominator, or both is called a *Complex Fraction*. These can be solved in a number of ways; with the simplest being by following the order of operations as stated earlier. For example, $\frac{\left(\frac{4}{7}\right)}{\left(\frac{5}{8}\right)} = \frac{0.571}{0.625} = 0.914$. Another way to solve this problem is to multiply the fraction in the numerator by the recipricol of the fraction in the denominator. For example, $\frac{\left(\frac{4}{7}\right)}{\left(\frac{5}{8}\right)} = \frac{4}{7} \times \frac{8}{5} = \frac{32}{35} = 0.914$.

> ➤ **Review Video: Fractions**
Visit **mometrix.com/academy** *and enter* **Code: 262335**

Percentages

Percentages can be thought of as fractions that are based on a whole of 100; that is, one whole is equal to 100%. The word percent means "per hundred." Fractions can be expressed as percents by finding equivalent fractions with a denomination of 100. Example: $\frac{7}{10} = \frac{70}{100} = 70\%$; $\frac{1}{4} = \frac{25}{100} = 25\%$.

To express a percentage as a fraction, divide the percentage number by 100 and reduce the fraction to its simplest possible terms. Example: $60\% = \frac{60}{100} = \frac{3}{5}$; $96\% = \frac{96}{100} = \frac{24}{25}$.

Converting decimals to percentages and percentages to decimals is as simple as moving the decimal point. To convert from a decimal to a percent, move the decimal point two places to the right. To convert from a percent to a decimal, move it two places to the left. Example: 0.23 = 23%; 5.34 = 534%; 0.007 = 0.7%; 700% = 7.00; 86% = 0.86; 0.15% = 0.0015. It may be helpful to remember that the percentage number will always be larger than the equivalent decimal number.

A percentage problem can be presented three main ways: (1) Find what percentage of some number another number is. Example: What percentage of 40 is 8? (2) Find what number is some percentage of a given number. Example: What number is 20% of 40? (3) Find what number another number is a given percentage of. Example: What number is 8 20% of? The three components in all of these cases are the same: a whole (W), a part (P), and a percentage (%). These are related by the equation: P = W × %. This is the form of the equation you would use to solve problems of type (2). To solve types (1) and (3), you would use these two forms: % = P/W and W = P/%.

The thing that frequently makes percentage problems difficult is that they are most often also word problems, so a large part of solving them is figuring out which quantities are what. Example: In a school cafeteria, 7 students choose pizza, 9 choose hamburgers, and 4 choose tacos. Find the percentage that chooses tacos. To find the whole, you must first add all of the parts: 7 + 9 + 4 = 20. The percentage can then be found by dividing the part by the whole (% = P/W): $\frac{4}{20} = \frac{20}{100} = 20\%$.

> **Review Video: <u>Percentages</u>**
Visit **mometrix.com/academy** and enter **Code: 141911**

Ratios

A ratio is a comparison of two quantities in a particular order. Example: If there are 14 computers in a lab, and the class has 20 students, there is a student to computer ratio of 20 to 14, commonly written as 20:14.

Two more comparisons used frequently in algebra are ratios and proportions. A *Ratio* is a comparison of two quantitites, expressed in a number of different ways. Ratios can be listed as "a to b", "a:b", or "a/b". Examples of ratios are miles per hour (miles/hour), meters per second (meters/second), miles per gallon (miles/gallon), etc..

> **Review Video: <u>Ratios</u>**
Visit **mometrix.com/academy** and enter **Code: 996914**

Proportions and Cross Products

A proportion is a relationship between two quantities that dictates how one changes when the other changes. A direct proportion describes a relationship in which a quantity increases by a set amount for every increase in the other quantity, or decreases by that same amount for every decrease in the other quantity. Example: For every 1 sheet cake, 18 people can be served cake. The number of sheet cakes, and the number of people that can be served from them is directly proportional.

A statement of two equal ratios is a *Proportion*, such as $\frac{m}{b} = \frac{w}{z}$. If Fred travels 2 miles in 1 hour and Jane travels 4 miles in 2 hours, their speeds are said to be proportional because $\frac{2}{1} = \frac{4}{2}$. In a proportion, the product of the numerator of the first ratio and the denominator of the second ratio is equal to the product of the denominator of the first ratio and the numerator of the second ratio. Using the previous example we see that $m \times z = b \times w$, thus $2 \times 2 = 1 \times 4$.

> **Review Video: <u>Proportions</u>**
Visit **mometrix.com/academy** and enter **Code: 505355**

Inverse proportion is a relationship in which an increase in one quantity is accompanied by a decrease in the other, or vice versa. Example: the time required for a car trip decreases as

- 7 -

the speed increases, and increases as the speed decreases, so the time required is inversely proportional to the speed of the car.

Scientific Notation

Scientific notation is a way of writing long numbers in a shorter form. The form $a \times 10^n$ is used in scientific notation. This form means that a is greater than or equal to 1 but less than 10. Also, n is the number of places the decimal must move to get from the original number to a.

Example: The number 230,400,000 is long to write. To see this value in scientific notation, place a decimal point between the first and second numbers. This includes all digits through the last non-zero digit ($a = 2.304$).

To find the correct power of 10, count the number of places the decimal point had to move ($n = 8$). The number is positive if the decimal moved to the left. Thus, the number is negative if it moved to the right. So, 230,400,000 can be written as 2.304×10^8.

Now, let's look at the number 0.00002304. We have the same value for a. However, this time the decimal moved 5 places to the right ($n = -5$). So, 0.00002304 can be written as 2.304×10^{-5}. This notation makes it easy to compare very large or very small numbers. By comparing exponents, you can see that 3.28×10^4 is smaller than 1.51×10^5 because 4 is less than 5.

Addition and Subtraction
To add and subtract numbers in scientific notation, you need the numbers to have the same power of 10. Next, you can add the constants. Then, you can use the power of 10 with the result.

If the constant is greater than 10 or less than 1, you need to move the decimal place. For constants less than 1, the decimal is moved to the right. For constants greater than 10, the decimal is moved to the left. Also, the power of 10 needs to change as you move the decimal place.

Example 1
In the problem $(4.8 \times 10^4) + (2.2 \times 10^4)$, the numbers have the same power of 10. So, add 4.8 and 2.2. So, you have 7 as the result. Now, the number can be written as (7×10^4).

Example 2
In the problem $(3.1 \times 10^8) - (2.4 \times 10^8)$, the numbers have the same power of 10. So, subtract 3.4 and 1.1. So, you have 0.7 as the result. Remember that you cannot have a constant that is less than 1. So, you need to move the decimal place one time to the right: (7×10^8). Also, the power of 10 has to change. Now, the number can be written as (7×10^{-1}).

The power of 10 is -1 because we moved the decimal place one time to the right. Now you have $(7 \times 10^{-1}) \times 10^8$. The reason is that we still have the power of 10 as 8. Now, you can add the -1 to the +8 for an answer of (7×10^7).

Example 3
In the problem$(5.3 \times 10^6) + (2.7 \times 10^7)$, the numbers do not have the same power of 10. So, you need one of the terms to have the same power. So, take (5.3×10^6) and change it to (0.53×10^7). Now, you can add 0.53 and 2.7. So, the number can be written as (3.23×10^7).

Multiplication
In the problem $(2.4 \times 10^3) \times (5.7 \times 10^5)$, you need to multiply 2.4 and 5.7. Then, you need to add the powers of 10 which are 3 and 5 for this example. So, you have (13.68×10^8). Remember that this cannot be an answer for scientific notation. The 13.68 for a constant is higher than 10. So, move the decimal to the left one time and change the exponent. Now, you have (1.368×10^9) as the answer.

Division
In the problem $(5.6 \times 10^6) \div (2.3 \times 10^2)$, you need to divide 5.6 and 2.3. Then, you need to subtract the powers of 10 which are 6 and 2 for this example. So, you have (2.43×10^4).

Permutation and Combination

When trying to calculate the probability of an event using the (desired outcomes)/(total outcomes formula), you may frequently find that there are too many outcomes to individually count them.

Permutation and combination formulas offer a shortcut to counting outcomes. The primary distinction between permutations and combinations is that permutations take into account order, while combinations do not. To calculate the number of possible groupings, there are two necessary parameters: the number of items available for selection and the number to be selected. The number of permutations of r items given a set of n items can be calculated as $_nP_r = \frac{n!}{(n-r)!}$. The number of combinations of r items given a set of n items can be calculated as $_nC_r = \frac{n!}{r!(n-r)!}$ or $_nC_r = \frac{_nP_r}{r!}$.

Example 1
Liz plays a game where she draws 6 cards from a deck of 52. How many combinations of cards can she draw?

To determine the number of combinations of 6 cards from a deck of 52, evaluate:
$$\frac{52!}{(52-6)!\,6!} = \frac{52 \cdot 51 \cdot 50 \cdot 49 \cdot 48 \cdot 47 \cdot 46!}{46!\,6!} =$$

$$\frac{52 \cdot 51 \cdot 50 \cdot 49 \cdot 48 \cdot 47}{6 \cdot 5 \cdot 4 \cdot 3 \cdot 2 \cdot 1} = \frac{13 \cdot 17 \cdot 10 \cdot 49 \cdot 4 \cdot 47}{1}$$

$$= 20358520$$

There are 20,358,520 combinations of cards that she can draw.

<u>Example 2</u>
Write the formula to compute the combination of r objects from a group of n objects. Twenty students are running for four class representative positions. Determine how many different combinations of four students can be selected from the twenty?

To determine the number of combinations of r objects from a total of n objects, use the formula: $_nC_r = \frac{n!}{(n-r)!\,r!}$

To determine the number of combinations of 4 students from 20, evaluate:

$$\frac{20!}{(20-4)!\,4!} = \frac{20 \cdot 19 \cdot 18 \cdot 17 \cdot 16!}{16!\,4!} =$$

$$\frac{20 \cdot 19 \cdot 18 \cdot 17}{4 \cdot 3 \cdot 2 \cdot 1} = \frac{5 \cdot 19 \cdot 3 \cdot 17}{1} = 4845$$

There are 4845 possible combinations of 4 students.

Factorials

The factorial is a function that can be performed on any non-negative integer. It is represented by the ! sign written after the integer on which it is being performed. The factorial of an integer is the product of all positive integers less than or equal to the number. For example, 4! (read "4 factorial") is calculated as $4 \times 3 \times 2 \times 1 = 24$.

Since 0 is not itself a positive integer, nor does it have any positive integers less than it, 0! cannot be calculated using this method. Instead, 0! is defined by convention to equal 1. This makes sense if you consider the pattern of descending factorials:

$$5! = 120$$
$$4! = \frac{5!}{5} = 24$$
$$3! = \frac{4!}{4} = 6$$
$$2! = \frac{3!}{3} = 2$$
$$1! = \frac{2!}{2} = 1$$
$$0! = \frac{1!}{1} = 1$$

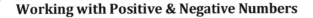

Algebra

Working with Positive & Negative Numbers

A precursor to working with negative numbers is understanding what absolute values are. A number's *Absolute Value* is simply the distance away from zero a number is on the number line. The absolute value of a number is always positive and is written $|x|$.

When adding signed numbers, if the signs are the same simply add the absolute values of the addends and apply the original sign to the sum. For example, $(+4) + (+8) = +12$ and $(-4) + (-8) = -12$. When the original signs are different, take the absolute values of the addends and subtract the smaller value from the larger value, then apply the original sign of the larger value to the difference. For instance, $(+4) + (-8) = -4$ and $(-4) + (+8) = +4$.

For subtracting signed numbers, change the sign of the number after the minus symbol and then follow the same rules used for addition. For example, $(+4) - (+8) = (+4) + (-8) = -4$.

If the signs are the same the product is positive when multiplying signed numbers. For example, $(+4) \times (+8) = +32$ and $(-4) \times (-8) = +32$. If the signs are opposite, the product is negative. For example, $(+4) \times (-8) = -32$ and $(-4) \times (+8) = -32$. When more than two factors are multiplied together, the sign of the product is determined by how many negative factors are present. If there are an odd number of negative factors then the product is negative, whereas an even number of negative factors indicates a positive product. For instance, $(+4) \times (-8) \times (-2) = +64$ and $(-4) \times (-8) \times (-2) = -64$.

The rules for dividing signed numbers are similar to multiplying signed numbers. If the dividend and divisor have the same sign, the quotient is positive. If the dividend and divisor have opposite signs, the quotient is negative. For example, $(-4) \div (+8) = -0.5$.

Exponent

An exponent is a superscript number placed next to another number at the top right. It indicates how many times the base number is to be multiplied by itself. Exponents provide a shorthand way to write what would be a longer mathematical expression. Example: $a^2 = a \times a$; $2^4 = 2 \times 2 \times 2 \times 2$. A number with an exponent of 2 is said to be "squared," while a number with an exponent of 3 is said to be "cubed." The value of a number raised to an exponent is called its power. So, 8^4 is read as "8 to the 4th power," or "8 raised to the power of 4." A negative exponent is the same as the reciprocal of a positive exponent. Example: $a^{-2} = 1/a^2$.

Laws of Exponents

The laws of exponents are as follows:
1) Any number to the power of 1 is equal to itself: $a^1 = a$.
2) The number 1 raised to any power is equal to 1: $1^n = 1$.
3) Any number raised to the power of 0 is equal to 1: $a^0 = 1$.
4) Add exponents to multiply powers of the same base number: $a^n \times a^m = a^{n+m}$.

5) Subtract exponents to divide powers of the same number; that is $a^n \div a^m = a^{n-m}$.

6) Multiply exponents to raise a power to a power: $(a^n)^m = a^{n \times m}$.

7) If multiplied or divided numbers inside parentheses are collectively raised to a power, this is the same as each individual term being raised to that power: $(a \times b)^n = a^n \times b^n$; $(a \div b)^n = a^n \div b^n$.

Note: Exponents do not have to be integers. Fractional or decimal exponents follow all the rules above as well. Example: $5^{\frac{1}{4}} \times 5^{\frac{3}{4}} = 5^{\frac{1}{4}+\frac{3}{4}} = 5^1 = 5$.

> ➤ **Review Video: Law of Exponents**
> Visit **mometrix.com/academy** and enter **Code: 532558**

Polynomial Algebra

Equations are made up of monomials and polynomials. A *Monomial* is a single variable or product of constants and variables, such as x, $2x$, or $\frac{2}{x}$. There will never be addition or subtraction symbols in a monomial. Like monomials have like variables, but they may have different coefficients. *Polynomials* are algebraic expressions which use addition and subtraction to combine two or more monomials. Two terms make a binomial; three terms make a trinomial; etc.. The *Degree of a Monomial* is the sum of the exponents of the variables. The *Degree of a Polynomial* is the highest degree of any individual term.

Add Polynomials

To add polynomials, you need to add like terms. These terms have the same variable part. An example is $4x^2$ and $3x^2$ have x^2 terms. To find the sum of like terms, find the sum of the coefficients. Then, keep the same variable part. You can use the distributive property to distribute the plus sign to each term of the polynomial. For example:

$(4x^2 - 5x + 7) + (3x^2 + 2x + 1) =$
$(4x^2 - 5x + 7) + 3x^2 + 2x + 1 =$
$(4x^2 + 3x^2) + (-5x + 2x) + (7 + 1) =$
$7x^2 - 3x + 8$

Subtract Polynomials

To subtract polynomials, you need to subtract like terms. To find the difference of like terms, find the difference of the coefficients. Then, keep the same variable part. You can use the distributive property to distribute the minus sign to each term of the polynomial. For example:

$(-2x^2 - x + 5) - (3x^2 - 4x + 1) =$
$(-2x^2 - x + 5) - 3x^2 + 4x - 1 =$
$(-2x^2 - 3x^2) + (-x + 4x) + (5 - 1) =$
$-5x^2 + 3x + 4$

Multiply Polynomials

To multiply two binomials, follow the *FOIL* method. FOIL stands for:

- First: Multiply the first term of each binomial
- Outer: Multiply the outer terms of each binomial
- Inner: Multiply the inner terms of each binomial
- Last: Multiply the last term of each binomial

Using FOIL $(Ax + By)(Cx + Dy) = ACx^2 + ADxy + BCxy + BDy^2$.

Example: $(3x + 6)(4x - 2)$
  First: $3x \times 4x = 12x^2$
  Outer: $3x \times -2 = -6x$ | Current Expression: $12x^2 - 6x$
  Inner: $6 \times 4x = 24x$ | Current Expression: $12x^2 - 6x + 24x$
  Last: $6 \times -2 = -12$ | Final Expression: $12x^2 - 6x + 24x - 12$

Now, combine like terms. For this example, that is $-6x + 24x$. Then, the expression looks like: $12x^2 + 18x - 12$. Each number is a multiple of 6. So, the expression becomes $6(2x^2 + 3x - 2)$, and the polynomial has been expanded.

Divide Polynomials

To divide polynomials, start with placing the terms of each polynomial in order of one variable. You may put them in ascending or descending order. Also, be consistent with both polynomials. To get the first term of the quotient, divide the first term of the dividend by the first term of the divisor. Next, multiply the first term of the quotient by the entire divisor. Then, subtract that product from the dividend and repeat for the following terms.

You want to end with a remainder of zero or a remainder with a degree that is less than the degree of the divisor. If the quotient has a remainder, write the answer as a mixed expression in the form: quotient $+ \frac{\text{remainder}}{\text{divisor}}$.

Example: Divide $4x^5 + 3x^2 - x$ by x

$$\frac{4x^5}{x} + \frac{3x^2}{x} - \frac{x}{x} = 4x^4 + 3x - 1$$

Below are patterns of some special products to remember: *perfect trinomial squares*, the *difference between two squares*, the *sum and difference of two cubes*, and *perfect cubes*.

- Perfect Trinomial Squares: $x^2 + 2xy + y^2 = (x + y)^2$ or $x^2 - 2xy + y^2 = (x - y)^2$
- Difference between Two Squares: $x^2 - y^2 = (x + y)(x - y)$
- Sum of Two Cubes: $x^3 + y^3 = (x + y)(x^2 - xy + y^2)$
  Note: the second factor is NOT the same as a perfect trinomial square. So, do not try to factor it further.
- Difference between Two Cubes: $x^3 - y^3 = (x - y)(x^2 + xy + y^2)$
  Again, the second factor is NOT the same as a perfect trinomial square.
- Perfect Cubes: $x^3 + 3x^2y + 3xy^2 + y^3 = (x + y)^3$ and $x^3 - 3x^2y + 3xy^2 - y^3 = (x - y)^3$

Factor a Polynomial

1. Check for a common monomial factor.
2. Factor out the greatest common monomial factor
3. Look for patterns of special products: differences of two squares, the sum or difference of two cubes for binomial factors, or perfect trinomial squares for trinomial factors.

Example
Solve the equation $2x^2 - 5x - 12 = 0$ by factoring.

The expression $2x^2 - 5x - 12$ splits into two factors of the form $(2x + a)(x + b)$. To find a and b, you must find two factors of -12 that sum to -5 after one of them is doubled.

-12 can be factored in the following ways: 1 and -12 | 2 and -6 | 3 and -4 |
4 and -3 | 6 and -2 | 12 and -1.

Of these factors, only 3 and -4 will sum to -5 after we double one of them. Since -4 is the factor that must be doubled, it should go in position b, where it will be multiplied by $2x$ when the FOIL method is used. The factored expression is $(2x + 3)(x - 4)$. So, you are left with $(2x + 3)(x - 4) = 0$.

By the zero product property, each value of x that will make one of the factors equal zero is a solution to this equation. The first factor equals zero when $x = -1.5$, and the second factor equals zero when $x = 4$. So, those are the solutions.

Note: The factor may be a trinomial but not a perfect trinomial square. So, look for a factorable form: $x^2 + (a + b)x + ab = (x + a)(x + b)$
or $(ac)x^2 + (ad + bc)x + bd = (ax + b)(cx + d)$

Some factors may have four terms. So, look for groups to factor. After you have found the factors, write the original polynomial as the product of all the factors. Make sure that all of the polynomial factors are prime. Monomial factors may be prime or composite. Check your work by multiplying the factors to make sure you get the original polynomial.

> ➤ **Review Video: Polynomials**
> *Visit **mometrix.com/academy** and enter **Code: 305005***

Inequalities

In algebra and higher areas of math, you will work with problems that do not equal each other. The statement comparing such expressions with symbols such as < (less than) or > (greater than) is called an *Inequality*.

One way to remember these symbols is to see that the sign for "less than" looks like an *L* for Less. Also, the sign for "greater than" looks like half of an *R* in g*R*eater. The terms *less than or equal to*, *at most*, or *no more than* are for the symbol ≤. Also, the terms *greater than or equal to*, *at least*, and *no less than* are for the symbol ≥.

Graphing and Solving Inequalities
Solving inequalities can be done with the same rules as for solving equations. However, when multiplying or dividing by a negative number, the direction of the inequality sign must be flipped or reversed.

Example 1
An example of an inequality is $7x > 5$. To solve for x, divide both sides by 7, and the solution is $x > \frac{5}{7}$. Graphs of the solution set of inequalities are given on a number line. Open circles are used to show that an expression approaches a number. However, the open circle points out that it is not equal to that number.

Example 2
Graph $10 > -2x + 4$.
In order to graph the inequality $10 > -2x + 4$, you need to solve for x. The opposite of addition is subtraction. So, subtract 4 from both sides. This gives you $6 > -2x$.

Next, the opposite of multiplication is division. So, divide both sides by -2. Don't forget to flip the inequality symbol because you are dividing by a negative number. Now, you have $-3 < x$. You can rewrite this as $x > -3$.

To graph an inequality, you make a number line. Then, put a circle around the value that is being compared to x. If you are graphing a *greater than* or *less than* inequality, the circle remains open. This stands for all of the values except -3. If the inequality is *greater than or equal to* or *less than or equal to*, you draw a closed circle around the value. This would stand for all of the values including the number.

Finally, look over the values that the solution stands for. Then, shade the number line in the needed direction. This example calls for graphing all of the values greater than -3. This is all of the numbers to the right of -3. So, you shade this area on the number line.

Other Inequalities
Conditional Inequalities are those with certain values for the variable that will make the condition true. So, other values for the variable where the condition will be false. *Absolute Inequalities* can have any real number as the value for the variable to make the condition true. So, there is no real number value for the variable that will make the condition false.

Double Inequalities are when two inequality statements are part of the same variable expression. An example of this is $-c < ax + b < c$.

Solving Quadratic Equations

The *Quadratic Formula* is used to solve quadratic equations when other methods are more difficult. To use the quadratic formula to solve a quadratic equation, begin by rewriting the equation in standard form $ax^2 + bx + c = 0$, where a, b, and c are coefficients. Once you have identified the values of the coefficients, substitute those values into the quadratic formula $= \frac{-b \pm \sqrt{b^2 - 4ac}}{2a}$. Evaluate the equation and simplify the expression. Again, check each root by substituting into the original equation. In the quadratic formula, the portion of the formula under the radical ($b^2 - 4ac$) is called the *Discriminant*. If the discriminant is zero, there is only one root: zero. If the discriminant is positive, there are two different real roots. If the discriminant is negative, there are no real roots.

To solve a quadratic equation by *Factoring*, begin by rewriting the equation in standard form, if necessary. Factor the side with the variable then set each of the factors equal to zero and solve the resulting linear equations. Check your answers by substituting the roots you found into the original equation. If, when writing the equation in standard form, you have an equation in the form $x^2 + c = 0$ or $x^2 - c = 0$, set $x^2 = -c$ or $x^2 = c$ and take the square root of c. If $c = 0$, the only real root is zero. If c is positive, there are two real roots—the positive and negative square root values. If c is negative, there are no real roots because you cannot take the square root of a negative number.

To solve a quadratic equation by *Completing the Square*, rewrite the equation so that all terms containing the variable are on the left side of the equal sign, and all the constants are on the right side of the equal sign. Make sure the coefficient of the squared term is 1. If there is a coefficient with the squared term, divide each term on both sides of the equal side by that number. Next, work with the coefficient of the single-variable term. Square half of this coefficient, and add that value to both sides. Now you can factor the left side (the side containing the variable) as the square of a binomial. $x^2 + 2ax + a^2 = C \Rightarrow (x + a)^2 = C$, where x is the variable, and a and C are constants. Take the square root of both sides and solve for the variable. Substitute the value of the variable in the original problem to check your work.

In order to solve a *Radical Equation*, begin by isolating the radical term on one side of the equation, and move all other terms to the other side of the equation. Look at the index of the radicand. Remember, if no number is given, the index is 2, meaning square root. Raise both sides of the equation to the power equal to the index of the radical. Solve the resulting equation as you would a normal polynomial equation. When you have found the roots, you must check them in the original problem to eliminate extraneous roots.

> ➤ **Review Video: <u>Using the Quadratic Formula</u>**
> *Visit **mometrix.com/academy** and enter **Code: 163102***

Geometry and Measurement

Lines and Planes

A point is a fixed location in space; has no size or dimensions; commonly represented by a dot.

A line is a set of points that extends infinitely in two opposite directions. It has length, but no width or depth. A line can be defined by any two distinct points that it contains. A line segment is a portion of a line that has definite endpoints. A ray is a portion of a line that extends from a single point on that line in one direction along the line. It has a definite beginning, but no ending.

A plane is a two-dimensional flat surface defined by three non-collinear points. A plane extends an infinite distance in all directions in those two dimensions. It contains an infinite number of points, parallel lines and segments, intersecting lines and segments, as well as parallel or intersecting rays. A plane will never contain a three-dimensional figure or skew lines. Two given planes will either be parallel or they will intersect to form a line. A plane may intersect a circular conic surface, such as a cone, to form conic sections, such as the parabola, hyperbola, circle or ellipse.

Perpendicular lines are lines that intersect at right angles. They are represented by the symbol ⊥. The shortest distance from a line to a point not on the line is a perpendicular segment from the point to the line.

Parallel lines are lines in the same plane that have no points in common and never meet. It is possible for lines to be in different planes, have no points in common, and never meet, but they are not parallel because they are in different planes.

A bisector is a line or line segment that divides another line segment into two equal lengths. A perpendicular bisector of a line segment is composed of points that are equidistant from the endpoints of the segment it is dividing.

Intersecting lines are lines that have exactly one point in common. Concurrent lines are multiple lines that intersect at a single point.

A transversal is a line that intersects at least two other lines, which may or may not be parallel to one another. A transversal that intersects parallel lines is a common occurrence in geometry.

Coordinate Plane

When algebraic functions and equations are shown graphically, they are usually shown on a *Cartesian Coordinate Plane*. The Cartesian coordinate plane consists of two number lines placed perpendicular to each other, and intersecting at the zero point, also known as the origin. The horizontal number line is known as the *x*-axis, with positive values to the right of the origin, and negative values to the left of the origin. The vertical number line is known as the *y*-axis, with positive values above the origin, and negative values below the origin.

Any point on the plane can be identified by an ordered pair in the form (x,y), called coordinates. The x-value of the coordinate is called the abscissa, and the y-value of the coordinate is called the ordinate. The two number lines divide the plane into four quadrants: I, II, III, and IV.

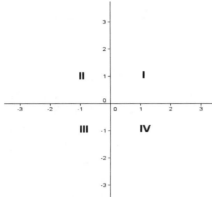

Before learning the different forms equations can be written in, it is important to understand some terminology. A ratio of the change in the vertical distance to the change in horizontal distance is called the *Slope*. On a graph with two points, (x_1, y_1) and (x_2, y_2), the slope is represented by the formula $= \frac{y_2 - y_1}{x_2 - x_1}$; $x_1 \neq x_2$. If the value of the slope is positive, the line slopes upward from left to right. If the value of the slope is negative, the line slopes downward from left to right. If the y-coordinates are the same for both points, the slope is 0 and the line is a *Horizontal Line*. If the x-coordinates are the same for both points, there is no slope and the line is a *Vertical Line*. Two or more lines that have equal slopes are *Parallel Lines*. *Perpendicular Lines* have slopes that are negative reciprocals of each other, such as $\frac{a}{b}$ and $\frac{-b}{a}$.

As mentioned previously, equations can be written many ways. Below is a list of the many forms equations can take.

- *Standard Form*: $Ax + By = C$; the slope is $\frac{-A}{B}$ and the y-intercept is $\frac{C}{B}$
- *Slope Intercept Form*: $y = mx + b$, where m is the slope and b is the y-intercept
- *Point-Slope Form*: $y - y_1 = m(x - x_1)$, where m is the slope and (x_1, y_1) is a point on the line
- *Two-Point Form*: $\frac{y - y_1}{x - x_1} = \frac{y_2 - y_1}{x_2 - x_1}$, where (x_1, y_1) and (x_2, y_2) are two points on the given line
- *Intercept Form*: $\frac{x}{x_1} + \frac{y}{y_1} = 1$, where $(x_1, 0)$ is the point at which a line intersects the x-axis, and $(0, y_1)$ is the point at which the same line intersects the y-axis

Equations can also be written as $ax + b = 0$, where $a \neq 0$. These are referred to as *One Variable Linear Equations*. A solution to an equation is called a *Root*. In the case where we have the equation $5x + 10 = 0$, if we solve for x we get a solution of $x = -2$. In other words, the root of the equation is -2. This is found by first subtracting 10 from both sides, which gives $5x = -10$. Next, simply divide both sides by the coefficient of the variable, in this case 5, to get $x = -2$. This can be checked by plugging -2 back into the original equation $(5)(-2) + 10 = -10 + 10 = 0$.

The *Solution Set* is the set of all solutions of an equation. In our example, the solution set would simply be -2. If there were more solutions (there usually are in multivariable equations) then they would also be included in the solution set. When an equation has no true solutions, this is referred to as an *Empty Set*. Equations with identical solution sets are *Equivalent Equations*. An *Identity* is a term whose value or determinant is equal to 1.

Calculations Using Points

Sometimes you need to perform calculations using only points on a graph as input data. Using points, you can determine what the midpoint and distance are. If you know the equation for a line you can calculate the distance between the line and the point.

To find the *Midpoint* of two points (x_1, y_1) and (x_2, y_2), average the x-coordinates to get the x-coordinate of the midpoint, and average the y-coordinates to get the y-coordinate of the midpoint. The formula is midpoint $= \left(\frac{x_1+x_2}{2}, \frac{y_1+y_2}{2}\right)$.

The *Distance* between two points is the same as the length of the hypotenuse of a right triangle with the two given points as endpoints, and the two sides of the right triangle parallel to the x-axis and y-axis, respectively. The length of the segment parallel to the x-axis is the difference between the x-coordinates of the two points. The length of the segment parallel to the y-axis is the difference between the y-coordinates of the two points. Use the Pythagorean Theorem $a^2 + b^2 = c^2$ or $c = \sqrt{a^2 + b^2}$ to find the distance. The formula is: distance $= \sqrt{(x_2 - x_1)^2 + (y_2 - y_1)^2}$.

When a line is in the format $Ax + By + C = 0$, where A, B, and C are coefficients, you can use a point (x_1, y_1) not on the line and apply the formula $d = \frac{|Ax_1 + By_1 + C|}{\sqrt{A^2 + B^2}}$ to find the distance between the line and the point (x_1, y_1).

> ➢ **Review Video: <u>Distance & Midpoint for Points on the Coordinate Plane</u>**
> *Visit **mometrix.com/academy** and enter **Code: 973653***

Transformation

- Rotation: An object is rotated, or turned, between 0 and 360 degrees, around a fixed point. The size and shape of the object are unchanged.
- Reflection: An object is reflected, or flipped, across a line, so that the original object and reflected object are the same distance from the line of reflection. The size and shape of the object are unchanged.
- Translation: An object is translated, or shifted, horizontally and/or vertically to a new location. The orientation, size, and shape of the object are unchanged.

Rotation

A line segment begins at (1, 4) and ends at (5, 4). Draw the line segment and rotate the line segment 90º about the point (3, 4).

The point about which the line segment is being rotated is on the line segment. This point should be on both the original and rotated line. The point (3, 4) is the center of the original line segment, and should still be the center of the rotated line segment. The dashed line is the rotated line segment.

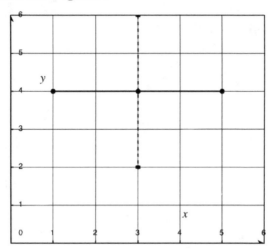

Reflection

Example 1: To create a congruent rectangle by reflecting, first draw a line of reflection. The line can be next to or on the figure. Then draw the image reflected across this line.

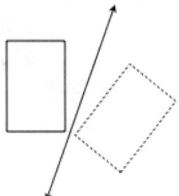

Example 2: A line segment begins at (1, 5) and ends at (5, 4). Draw the line segment, then reflect the line segment across the line $y = 3$.

To reflect a segment, consider folding a piece of paper at the line of reflection. The new image should line up exactly with the old image when the paper is folded. The dashed line is the reflected line segment.

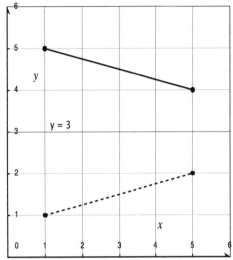

Translation

Example 1: A line segment on an x-y grid starts at (3, 2) and ends at (4, 1). Draw the line segment, and translate the segment up 2 units and left 2 units.

The solid line segment is the original line segment, and the dashed line is the translated line segment. The *y*-coordinate of each point has increased by 2, because the points moved two units away from 0. The *x*-coordinate of each point has decreased by 2, because the points moved two units closer to 0.

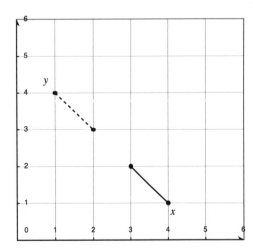

Example 2: Identify a transformation that could have been performed on the solid triangle to result in the dashed triangle.

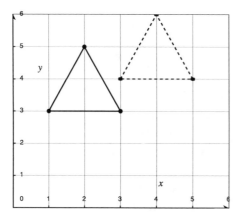

The transformed triangle has the same orientation as the original triangle. It has been shifted up one unit and two units to the right. Because the orientation of the figure has not changed, and its new position can be described using shifts up and to the right, the figure was translated.

Angles

An angle is formed when two lines or line segments meet at a common point. It may be a common starting point for a pair of segments or rays, or it may be the intersection of lines. Angles are represented by the symbol ∠.

The vertex is the point at which two segments or rays meet to form an angle. If the angle is formed by intersecting rays, lines, and/or line segments, the vertex is the point at which four angles are formed. The pairs of angles opposite one another are called vertical angles, and their measures are equal.

An acute angle is an angle with a degree measure less than 90°.
A right angle is an angle with a degree measure of exactly 90°.
An obtuse angle is an angle with a degree measure greater than 90° but less than 180°.
A straight angle is an angle with a degree measure of exactly 180°. This is also a semicircle.
A reflex angle is an angle with a degree measure greater than 180° but less than 360°.
A full angle is an angle with a degree measure of exactly 360°.

> ➤ **Review Video: Angles**
> *Visit* ***mometrix.com/academy*** *and enter* ***Code: 264624***

Two angles whose sum is exactly 90° are said to be complementary. The two angles may or may not be adjacent. In a right triangle, the two acute angles are complementary.

Two angles whose sum is exactly 180° are said to be supplementary. The two angles may or may not be adjacent. Two intersecting lines always form two pairs of supplementary angles. Adjacent supplementary angles will always form a straight line.

Two angles that have the same vertex and share a side are said to be adjacent. Vertical angles are not adjacent because they share a vertex but no common side.

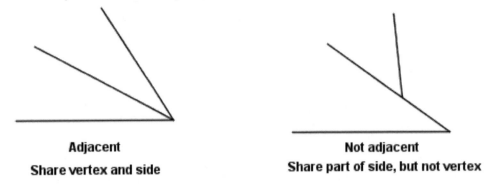

Adjacent

Share vertex and side

Not adjacent

Share part of side, but not vertex

When two parallel lines are cut by a transversal, the angles that are between the two parallel lines are interior angles. In the diagram below, angles 3, 4, 5, and 6 are interior angles.

When two parallel lines are cut by a transversal, the angles that are outside the parallel lines are exterior angles. In the diagram below, angles 1, 2, 7, and 8 are exterior angles.

When two parallel lines are cut by a transversal, the angles that are in the same position relative to the transversal and a parallel line are corresponding angles. The diagram below has four pairs of corresponding angles: angles 1 and 5; angles 2 and 6; angles 3 and 7; and angles 4 and 8. Corresponding angles formed by parallel lines are congruent.

When two parallel lines are cut by a transversal, the two interior angles that are on opposite sides of the transversal are called alternate interior angles. In the diagram below, there are two pairs of alternate interior angles: angles 3 and 6, and angles 4 and 5. Alternate interior angles formed by parallel lines are congruent.

When two parallel lines are cut by a transversal, the two exterior angles that are on opposite sides of the transversal are called alternate exterior angles. In the diagram below, there are two pairs of alternate exterior angles: angles 1 and 8, and angles 2 and 7. Alternate exterior angles formed by parallel lines are congruent.

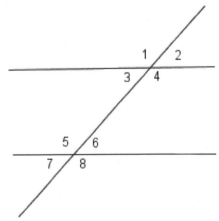

When two lines intersect, four angles are formed. The non-adjacent angles at this vertex are called vertical angles. Vertical angles are congruent. In the diagram, $\angle ABD \cong \angle CBE$ and $\angle ABC \cong \angle DBE$.

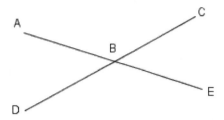

Triangles

An equilateral triangle is a triangle with three congruent sides. An equilateral triangle will also have three congruent angles, each 60°. All equilateral triangles are also acute triangles.

An isosceles triangle is a triangle with two congruent sides. An isosceles triangle will also have two congruent angles opposite the two congruent sides.

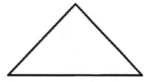

A scalene triangle is a triangle with no congruent sides. A scalene triangle will also have three angles of different measures. The angle with the largest measure is opposite the longest side, and the angle with the smallest measure is opposite the shortest side.

An acute triangle is a triangle whose three angles are all less than 90°. If two of the angles are equal, the acute triangle is also an isosceles triangle. If the three angles are all equal, the acute triangle is also an equilateral triangle.

A right triangle is a triangle with exactly one angle equal to 90°. All right triangles follow the Pythagorean Theorem. A right triangle can never be acute or obtuse.

An obtuse triangle is a triangle with exactly one angle greater than 90°. The other two angles may or may not be equal. If the two remaining angles are equal, the obtuse triangle is also an isosceles triangle.

Triangle Terminology

Altitude of a Triangle: A line segment drawn from one vertex perpendicular to the opposite side. In the diagram below, $\overline{BE}$, $\overline{AD}$, and $\overline{CF}$ are altitudes. The three altitudes in a triangle are always concurrent.

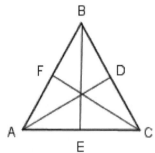

Height of a Triangle: The length of the altitude, although the two terms are often used interchangeably.

Orthocenter of a Triangle: The point of concurrency of the altitudes of a triangle. Note that in an obtuse triangle, the orthocenter will be outside the triangle, and in a right triangle, the orthocenter is the vertex of the right angle.

Median of a Triangle: A line segment drawn from one vertex to the midpoint of the opposite side. This is not the same as the altitude, except the altitude to the base of an isosceles triangle and all three altitudes of an equilateral triangle.

Centroid of a Triangle: The point of concurrency of the medians of a triangle. This is the same point as the orthocenter only in an equilateral triangle. Unlike the orthocenter, the centroid is always inside the triangle. The centroid can also be considered the exact center of the triangle. Any shape triangle can be perfectly balanced on a tip placed at the centroid. The centroid is also the point that is two-thirds the distance from the vertex to the opposite side.

> **Review Video: Incenter, Circumcenter, Orthocenter, and Centroid**
> *Visit mometrix.com/academy and enter Code: 598260*

General Rules for Triangles

The Triangle Inequality Theorem states that the sum of the measures of any two sides of a triangle is always greater than the measure of the third side. If the sum of the measures of two sides were equal to the third side, a triangle would be impossible because the two sides would lie flat across the third side and there would be no vertex. If the sum of the measures of two of the sides was less than the third side, a closed figure would be impossible because the two shortest sides would never meet.

The sum of the measures of the interior angles of a triangle is always 180°. Therefore, a triangle can never have more than one angle greater than or equal to 90°.

In any triangle, the angles opposite congruent sides are congruent, and the sides opposite congruent angles are congruent. The largest angle is always opposite the longest side, and the smallest angle is always opposite the shortest side.

The line segment that joins the midpoints of any two sides of a triangle is always parallel to the third side and exactly half the length of the third side.

Pythagorean Theorem

The side of a triangle opposite the right angle is called the hypotenuse. The other two sides are called the legs. The Pythagorean Theorem states a relationship among the legs and hypotenuse of a right triangle: $a^2 + b^2 = c^2$, where a and b are the lengths of the legs of a right triangle, and c is the length of the hypotenuse. Note that this formula will only work with right triangles.

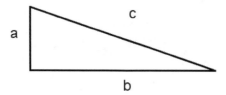

➢ **Review Video: Pythagorean Theorem**
*Visit **mometrix.com/academy** and enter **Code: 906576***

Polygons

Each straight line segment of a polygon is called a side.

The point at which two sides of a polygon intersect is called the vertex. In a polygon, the number of sides is always equal to the number of vertices.

A polygon with all sides congruent and all angles equal is called a regular polygon.

A line segment from the center of a polygon perpendicular to a side of the polygon is called the apothem. In a regular polygon, the apothem can be used to find the area of the polygon using the formula $A = \frac{1}{2}ap$, where a is the apothem and p is the perimeter.

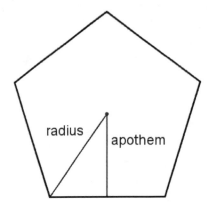

A line segment from the center of a polygon to a vertex of the polygon is called a radius. The radius of a regular polygon is also the radius of a circle that can be circumscribed about the polygon.

Triangle – 3 sides
Quadrilateral – 4 sides
Pentagon – 5 sides
Hexagon – 6 sides
Heptagon – 7 sides
Octagon – 8 sides
Nonagon – 9 sides
Decagon – 10 sides
Dodecagon – 12 sides

More generally, an n-gon is a polygon that has n angles and n sides.

Quadrilateral: A closed two-dimensional geometric figure composed of exactly four straight sides. The sum of the interior angles of any quadrilateral is 360°.

Parallelogram: A quadrilateral that has exactly two pairs of opposite parallel sides. The sides that are parallel are also congruent. The opposite interior angles are always congruent, and the consecutive interior angles are supplementary. The diagonals of a parallelogram bisect each other. Each diagonal divides the parallelogram into two congruent triangles.

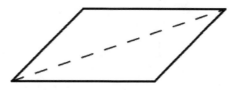

Trapezoid: Traditionally, a quadrilateral that has exactly one pair of parallel sides. Some math texts define trapezoid as a quadrilateral that has at least one pair of parallel sides. Because there are no rules governing the second pair of sides, there are no rules that apply to the properties of the diagonals of a trapezoid.

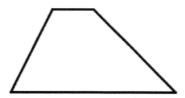

Rectangles, rhombuses, and squares are all special forms of parallelograms.
Rectangle: A parallelogram with four right angles. All rectangles are parallelograms, but not all parallelograms are rectangles. The diagonals of a rectangle are congruent.

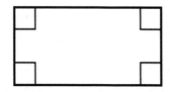

Rhombus: A parallelogram with four congruent sides. All rhombuses are parallelograms, but not all parallelograms are rhombuses. The diagonals of a rhombus are perpendicular to each other.

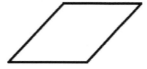

Square: A parallelogram with four right angles and four congruent sides. All squares are also parallelograms, rhombuses, and rectangles. The diagonals of a square are congruent and perpendicular to each other.

A quadrilateral whose diagonals bisect each other is a parallelogram. A quadrilateral whose opposite sides are parallel (2 pairs of parallel sides) is a parallelogram.

A quadrilateral whose diagonals are perpendicular bisectors of each other is a rhombus. A quadrilateral whose opposite sides (both pairs) are parallel and congruent is a rhombus.

A parallelogram that has a right angle is a rectangle. (Consecutive angles of a parallelogram are supplementary. Therefore if there is one right angle in a parallelogram, there are four right angles in that parallelogram.)

A rhombus with one right angle is a square. Because the rhombus is a special form of a parallelogram, the rules about the angles of a parallelogram also apply to the rhombus.

Circles

The center is the single point inside the circle that is equidistant from every point on the circle. (Point O in the diagram below.)

The radius is a line segment that joins the center of the circle and any one point on the circle. All radii of a circle are equal. (Segments OX, OY, and OZ in the diagram below.)

The diameter is a line segment that passes through the center of the circle and has both endpoints on the circle. The length of the diameter is exactly twice the length of the radius. (Segment XZ in the diagram below.)

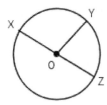

Area and Perimeter Formulas

<u>Triangle</u>
The perimeter of any triangle is found by summing the three side lengths; $P = a + b + c$. For an equilateral triangle, this is the same as $P = 3s$, where s is any side length, since all three sides are the same length.

Find the side of a triangle
You may have problems that give you the perimeter of a triangle. So, you are asked to find one of the sides.

Example: The perimeter of a triangle is 35 cm. One side length is 10 cm. Another side length is 20cm. Find the length of the missing side.

    First: Set up the equation to set apart a side length.
          Now, the equation is $35 = 10 + 20 + c$. So, you are left with $35 = 30 + c$.

    Second: Subtract 30 from both sides: $35 - 30 = 30 - 30 + c$
          Then, you are left with $5 = c$

The area of any triangle can be found by taking half the product of one side length (base or b) and the perpendicular distance from that side to the opposite vertex (height or h). In equation form, $A = \frac{1}{2}bh$. For many triangles, it may be difficult to calculate h, so using one of the other formulas given here may be easier.

Find the height or the area of the base
You may have problems that give you the area of a triangle. So, you are asked to find the height or the base.

Example: The area of a triangle is 70 cm², and the height is 10. Find the base.
    First: Set up the equation to set apart the base.
          The equation is $70 = \frac{1}{2}10b$.
          Now, multiply both sides by 2: $70 \times 2 = \frac{1}{2}10b \times 2$.
          So, you are left with: $140 = 10b$.

    Second: Divide both sides by 10 to get the base: $\frac{140}{10} = \frac{10b}{10}$
          Then, you have $14 = b$.

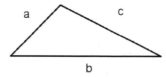

> ➤ **Review Video: <u>Area and Perimeter of a Triangle</u>**
> *Visit **mometrix.com/academy** and enter **Code: 853779***

Another formula that works for any triangle is $A = \sqrt{s(s-a)(s-b)(s-c)}$, where A is the area, s is the semiperimeter $s = \frac{a+b+c}{2}$, and a, b, and c are the lengths of the three sides.

The area of an equilateral triangle can be found by the formula $A = \frac{\sqrt{3}}{4} s^2$, where A is the area and s is the length of a side. You could use the $30° - 60° - 90°$ ratios to find the height of the triangle and then use the standard triangle area formula, but this is faster.

The area of an isosceles triangle can be found by the formula, $A = \frac{1}{2} b \sqrt{a^2 - \frac{b^2}{4}}$, where A is the area, b is the base (the unique side), and a is the length of one of the two congruent sides. If you do not remember this formula, you can use the Pythagorean Theorem to find the height so you can use the standard formula for the area of a triangle.

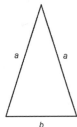

Square
The area of a square is found by using the formula $A = s^2$, where and s is the length of one side.

Find the side of a square
You may have problems that give you the area of a square. So, you are asked to find the side.
Example: The area of a square is 9 cm². Find the side.
    First: Set up the equation to set apart s.
           The equation is $9 = s^2$.

    Second: Now, you can take the square root of both sides: $\sqrt{9} = \sqrt{s^2}$.
           So, you are left with: $3 = s$

The perimeter of a square is found by using the formula $P = 4s$, where s is the length of one side. Because all four sides are equal in a square, it is faster to multiply the length of one side by 4 than to add the same number four times. You could use the formulas for rectangles and get the same answer.

Find the side of a square
You may have problems that give you the perimeter of a square. So, you are asked to find the side.
Example: The perimeter of a square is 60 cm. Find the side.
    First: Set up the equation to set apart s.
           The equation is $60 = 4s$.

    Second: Now, you can divide both sides by 4: $\frac{60}{4} = \frac{4s}{4}$. You are left with $15 = s$

➢ **Review Video: <u>Area and Perimeter of a Square</u>**
*Visit **mometrix.com/academy** and enter **Code: 620902***

Rectangle

The area of a rectangle is found by the formula $A = lw$, where A is the area of the rectangle, l is the length (usually considered to be the longer side) and w is the width (usually considered to be the shorter side). The numbers for l and w are interchangeable.

Find the width or length of a rectangle
You may have problems that give you the area of a rectangle. So, you are asked to find the width.
Example: The area of a rectangle is 150cm², and the length is 10cm. Find the width.

First: Set up the equation to set apart width. The equation is $150 = 10w$.

Second: Divide both sides by 10: $\frac{150}{10} = \frac{10w}{10}$. You are left with $15 = w$

Note: When you need to find the length, you can follow the steps above to find it.

The perimeter of a rectangle is found by the formula $P = 2l + 2w$ or $P = 2(l + w)$, where l is the length, and w is the width. It may be easier to add the length and width first and then double the result, as in the second formula.

Find the width or length of a rectangle
You may have problems that give you the perimeter of a rectangle. So, you are asked to find the width.
Example: The perimeter of a rectangle is 100cm, and the length is 20cm. Find the width.

First: Set up the equation to set apart the width. The equation is $100 = 2(20 + w)$

Second: Distribute the 2 across $(20 + w)$: $100 = 40 + 2w$
Then, subtract 40 from both sides: $100 - 40 = 40 + 2w - 40$
So, you are left with: $60 = 2w$. Then, divide both sides by 2: $\frac{60}{2} = \frac{2w}{2}$.
Now, you have $30 = w$.

Note: When you need to find the length, you can follow the steps above to find it.

> ➢ **Review Video: <u>Area and Perimeter of a Rectangle</u>**
> *Visit **mometrix.com/academy** and enter **Code: 933707***

Parallelogram

The area of a parallelogram is found by the formula $A = bh$, where b is the length of the base, and h is the height. Note that the base and height correspond to the length and width in a rectangle, so this formula would apply to rectangles as well. Do not confuse the height of a parallelogram with the length of the second side. The two are only the same measure in the case of a rectangle.

Find the length of the base or the height of a parallelogram
You may have problems that give you the area of a parallelogram. So, you are asked to find the area of the base or the height.
Example: The area of the parallelogram is 84 cm². The base is 7cm. Find the height.

Set up the equation to set apart the height.

So, you have $84 = 7h$. Now, divide both sides by 7: $\frac{84}{7} = \frac{7h}{7}$.
Then, you are left with $12 = h$

The perimeter of a parallelogram is found by the formula $P = 2a + 2b$ or $P = 2(a + b)$, where a and b are the lengths of the two sides.

Find the missing side of a parallelogram
You may have problems that give you the perimeter of a parallelogram. So, you are asked to find one of the sides. Example: The perimeter of a parallelogram is 100cm, and one side is 20cm. Find the other side.

First: Set up the equation to set apart one of the side lengths.
The equation is $100 = 2(20 + b)$

Second: Distribute the 2 across $(20 + b)$: $100 = 40 + 2b$
Then, subtract 40 from both sides: $100 - 40 = 40 + 2b - 40$
So, you are left with: $60 = 2b$. Then, divide both sides by 2: $\frac{60}{2} = \frac{2b}{2}$
Now, you have $30 = b$.

> ➤ **Review Video: <u>Area and Perimeter of a Parallelogram</u>**
> *Visit **mometrix.com/academy** and enter **Code: 718313***

<u>Trapezoid</u>
The area of a trapezoid is found by the formula $A = \frac{1}{2}h(b_1 + b_2)$, where h is the height (segment joining and perpendicular to the parallel bases), and b_1 and b_2 are the two parallel sides (bases). Do not use one of the other two sides as the height unless that side is also perpendicular to the parallel bases.

Find the height of a trapezoid
You may have problems that give you the area of a trapezoid. So, you are asked to find the height.
Example: The area of a trapezoid is 30cm². B_1 is 3cm, and B_2 is 9cm. Find the height.

First: Set up the equation to set apart the height. The equation is $30 = \frac{1}{2}h(3 + 9)$.

Second: Now, multiply both sides by 2: $30 \times 2 = \frac{1}{2}(12)h \times 2$.
So, you are left with: $60 = (12)h$.

Third: Divide both sides by 12: $\frac{60}{12} = \frac{(12)h}{12}$. Now, you have $5 = h$

Find a base of a trapezoid
You may have problems that give you the area of a trapezoid and the height. So, you are asked to find one of the bases.
Example: The area of a trapezoid is 90cm². b_1 is 5cm, and the height is 12cm. Find b_2.

First: Set up the equation to set apart b_2.
The equation is $90 = \frac{1}{2}12(5 + b_2)$.

Second: Now, multiply the height by $\frac{1}{2}$: $90 = 6(5 + b_2)$.
So, you can distribute the 6 across $(5 + b_2)$: $90 = 30 + 6b_2$

Third: Subtract 30 from both sides $90 - 30 = 30 + 6b_2 - 30$.
Now, you have $60 = 6b_2$.
Then, divide both sides by 6: $\frac{60}{6} = \frac{6b_2}{6}$. So, $b_2 = 10$.

The perimeter of a trapezoid is found by the formula $P = a + b_1 + c + b_2$, where $a, b_1, c,$ and b_2 are the four sides of the trapezoid.

Find the missing side of a trapezoid
Example: The perimeter of a trapezoid is 50cm. B_1 is 20cm, B_2 is 10cm, and a is 5cm. Find the length of side c.

First: Set up the equation to set apart the missing side.
The equation is $50 = 5 + 20 + c + 10$. So, you have $50 = 35 + c$

Second: Subtract 35 from both sides: $50 - 35 = 35 + c - 35$.
So, you are left with $15 = c$

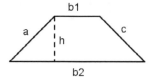

> ➢ **Review Video: <u>Area and Perimeter of a Trapezoid</u>**
> *Visit **mometrix.com/academy** and enter **Code: 587523***

<u>Circles</u>
The area of a circle is found by the formula $A = \pi r^2$, where r is the length of the radius. If the diameter of the circle is given, remember to divide it in half to get the length of the radius before proceeding.

Find the radius of a circle
You may have problems that give you the area of a circle. So, you are asked to find the radius.
Example: The area of a circle is 30cm². Find the radius.

First: Set up the equation to set apart the radius.
The equation is $30 = \pi r^2$. Now, divide both sides by π: $\dfrac{30}{\pi} = \dfrac{\pi r^2}{\pi}$

Second: Take the square root of both sides: $\sqrt{9.55} = \sqrt{r^2}$.
So, you are left with: $3.09 = r$.

Note: You may have the area, and you are asked to find the diameter of the circle. So, follow the steps above to find the radius. Then, multiply the radius by 2 for the diameter.

The circumference of a circle is found by the formula $C = 2\pi r$, where r is the radius. Again, remember to convert the diameter if you are given that measure rather than the radius.

Find the radius of a circle
You may have problems that give you the circumference of a circle. So, you are asked to find the radius. Example: The circumference is 20cm. Find the radius.

    First: Set up the equation to set apart the radius.

        The equation is $20 = 2\pi r$. Now divide both sides by 2: $\frac{20}{2} = \frac{2\pi r}{2}$.

    Second: Divide both sides by π: $\frac{10}{\pi} = \frac{\pi r}{\pi}$. So, you are left with $3.18 = r$

Note: You may have the circumference, and you are asked to find the diameter of the circle. So, follow the steps above to find the radius. Then, multiply the radius by 2 for the diameter.

> ➤ **Review Video: <u>Area and Circumference of a Circle</u>**
> *Visit **mometrix.com/academy** and enter **Code: 243015***

Volume and Surface Area

The surface area of a solid object is the area of all sides or exterior surfaces. For objects such as prisms and pyramids, a further distinction is made between base surface area (B) and lateral surface area (LA). For a prism, the total surface area (SA) is $SA = LA + 2B$. For a pyramid or cone, the total surface area is $SA = LA + B$.

<u>Rectangular Prism</u>

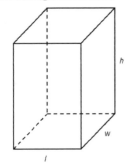

For a rectangular prism, the volume can be found by the formula $V = lwh$, where V is the volume, l is the length, w is the width, and h is the height.

Find the length, width, or height of a rectangular prism
You may have problems that give you the volume of a rectangular prism. So, you are asked to find the length, width, or height.
Example: The volume of the rectangular prism is 200 cm³. The width is 10cm, and the height is 10cm. Find the length.

    First: Set up the equation to set apart the length.

        So, you have $200 = l(10)(10)$ that becomes $200 = (100)l$.

    Second: Divide both sides by 100.

        Now, you have $\frac{200}{100} = \frac{(100)l}{100}$. So, you are left with $2 = l$.

Note: When you need to find the width or height, you can follow the steps above to solve for either.

The surface area can be calculated as $SA = 2lw + 2hl + 2wh$ or $SA = 2(lw + hl + wh)$.

Find the length, width, or height of a rectangular prism
You may have problems that give you the surface area of a rectangular prism. So, you are asked to find the length, width, or height.
Example: The surface area of the rectangular prism is 200 cm². The width is 15cm, and the height is 5cm. Find the length.

First: Set up the equation to set apart the length.
So, you have $200 = 2(15)l + 2(5)l + 2(15)(5)$ that becomes:
$200 = (40)l + 150$.

Second: Subtract 150 from both sides.
So, $200 - 150 = (40)l + 150 - 150$ becomes $50 = (40)l$.
Then, divide both sides by 40 to set apart l: $\frac{50}{40} = \frac{(40)l}{40}$.
You are left with $1.25 = l$.

Note: When you need to find the width or height, you can follow the steps above to solve for either.

<u>Cube</u>
The volume of a cube can be found by the formula $V = s^3$, where s is the length of a side.

Find the side of a cube
You may have problems that give you the volume of a cube. So, you are asked to find the side.
Example: The volume of a cube is 20 cm³. Find the side.

First: Set up the equation to set apart the side length. Then, take the cube root of both sides. So, $20 = s^3$ becomes $\sqrt[3]{20} = \sqrt[3]{s^3}$ Then, you are left with $\sqrt[3]{20} = s$

Second: Solve for the side length.
$\sqrt[3]{20} = 2.71$. So, s equals 2.71.

The surface area of a cube is calculated as $SA = 6s^2$, where SA is the total surface area and s is the length of a side. These formulas are the same as the ones used for the volume and surface area of a rectangular prism, but simplified since all three quantities (length, width, and height) are the same.

Find the side of a cube
You may have problems that give you the surface area of a cube. So, you are asked to find the side.
Example: The surface area of a cube is 60 cm². Find the side.

First: Set up the equation to set apart the side length.
So, $60 = 6s^2$ becomes $\frac{60}{6} = \frac{6s^2}{6}$. Then, you are left with $10 = s^2$

Second: Take the square root of both sides to set apart the s.
So, $10 = s^2$ becomes $\sqrt{10} = \sqrt{s^2}$.
Then, you are left with $3.16 = s$

➤ **Review Video: <u>Volume and Surface Area of a Rectangular Solid</u>**
*Visit **mometrix.com/academy** and enter **Code: 386780***

<u>Cylinder</u>

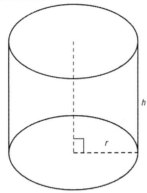

The volume of a cylinder can be calculated by the formula $V = \pi r^2 h$, where r is the radius, and h is the height.

Find the height of a cylinder
You may have problems that give you the volume of a cylinder. So, you are asked to find the height.
Example: The volume of a cylinder is 300 cm³ and the radius is 5 cm. Find the height.

    First: Set up the equation and put in the known numbers.
        You begin with $300 = \pi 5^2 h$. Now, $\pi 5^2 h = 78.5h$.
        So, you have $300 = 78.5h$

    Second: Set apart h to solve for the height.
        $\frac{300}{78.5} = \frac{78.5h}{78.5}$. So, you are left with: $\frac{300}{78.5} = h$

        Solve: $\frac{300}{78.5} = 3.82$cm is the height.

Find the radius of a cylinder
You may have problems that give you the volume of a cylinder. So, you are asked to find the radius.
Example: The volume of a cylinder is 200 cm³ and the radius is 15cm. Find the radius.

    First: Set up the equation to set apart the radius.
        You begin with $200 = \pi(15)r^2$. Now, you move π and (15) to both sides of
        the equation: $\frac{200}{\pi(15)} = \frac{\pi(15)r^2}{\pi(15)}$. Then, you are left with: $\frac{200}{\pi(15)} = r^2$.

    Second: Take the square root of both sides to solve for the radius: $\sqrt{\frac{200}{\pi(15)}} = \sqrt{r^2}$.

        Then, you have $\sqrt{4.25} = r$. So, the radius is equal to 2.06.

The surface area of a cylinder can be found by the formula $SA = 2\pi r^2 + 2\pi rh$. The first term is the base area multiplied by two, and the second term is the perimeter of the base multiplied by the height.

Find the height of a cylinder

You may have problems that give you the surface area of a cylinder. So, you are asked to find the height. Example: The surface area of a cylinder is 150 cm² and the radius is 2 cm. Find the height.

First: Set up the equation and put in the known numbers.
You begin with $150 = 2\pi 2^2 + 2\pi(2)h$.
So, you have $150 = 25.12 + 12.56h$.

Second: Subtract 25.12 from both sides of the equation.
So, $150 - 25.12 = 25.12 + 12.56h - 25.12$ becomes $124.85 = 12.56h$.
Then, divide both sides by 12.56.
Now, you are left with $9.94 = h$.

Find the radius of a cylinder

You may have problems that give you the surface area of a cylinder. So, you are asked to find the radius. Example: The surface area of a cylinder is 327 cm², and the height is 12cm. Find the radius.

First: Set up the equation and put in the known numbers.
You begin with $327 = 2\pi r^2 + 2\pi 12(r)$. So, you have $327 = 2\pi r^2 + 75.36r$.

Second: Set up the quadratic formula.
So, you now have $6.28r^2 + 75.36r - 327 = 0$

Third: Solve the equation using the quadratic formula steps.
Now, radius $= \dfrac{-75.36 \pm \sqrt{(75.36)^2 - 4(6.28)(-327)}}{2(6.28)}$
So, the radius equals a positive 3.39.

➢ **Review Video: <u>Volume and Surface Area of a Right Circular Cylinder</u>**
*Visit **mometrix.com/academy** and enter **Code: 226463***

Data Analysis and Probability

Measures of Central Tendency

The quantities of mean, median, and mode are all referred to as measures of central tendency. They can each give a picture of what the whole set of data looks like with just a single number. Knowing what each of these values represents is vital to making use of the information they provide.

The mean, also known as the arithmetic mean or average, of a data set is calculated by summing all of the values in the set and dividing that sum by the number of values. For example, if a data set has 6 numbers and the sum of those 6 numbers is 30, the mean is calculated as 30/6 = 5.

The median is the middle value of a data set. The median can be found by putting the data set in numerical order, and locating the middle value. In the data set (1, 2, 3, 4, 5), the median is 3. If there is an even number of values in the set, the median is calculated by taking the average of the two middle values. In the data set, (1, 2, 3, 4, 5, 6), the median would be (3 + 4)/2 = 3.5.

The mode is the value that appears most frequently in the data set. In the data set (1, 2, 3, 4, 5, 5, 5), the mode would be 5 since the value 5 appears three times. If multiple values appear the same number of times, there are multiple values for the mode. If the data set were (1, 2, 2, 3, 4, 4, 5, 5), the modes would be 2, 4, and 5. If no value appears more than any other value in the data set, then there is no mode.

Measures of Dispersion

The standard deviation expresses how spread out the values of a distribution are from the mean. Standard deviation is given in the same units as the original data and is represented by a lower case sigma (σ). A high standard deviation means that the values are very spread out. A low standard deviation means that the values are close together.

If every value in a distribution is increased or decreased by the same amount, the mean, median, and mode are increased or decreased by that amount, but the standard deviation stays the same. If every value in a distribution is multiplied or divided by the same number, the mean, median, mode, and standard deviation will all be multiplied or divided by that number.

The range of a distribution is the difference between the highest and lowest values in the distribution. For example, in the data set (1, 3, 5, 7, 9, 11), the highest and lowest values are 11 and 1, respectively. The range then would be calculated as 11 – 1 = 10.

The three quartiles are the three values that divide a data set into four equal parts. Quartiles are generally only calculated for data sets with a large number of values. As a simple example, for the data set consisting of the numbers 1 through 99, the first quartile (Q1) would be 25, the second quartile (Q2), always equal to the median, would be 50, and the third quartile (Q3) would be 75. The difference between Q1 and Q3 is known as the interquartile range.

Probability

Probability is a branch of statistics that deals with the likelihood of something taking place. One classic example is a coin toss. There are only two possible results: heads or tails. The likelihood, or probability, that the coin will land as heads is 1 out of 2 (1/2, 0.5, 50%). Tails has the same probability. Another common example is a 6-sided die roll. There are six possible results from rolling a single die, each with an equal chance of happening, so the probability of any given number coming up is 1 out of 6.

> ➢ **Review Video: <u>Simple Probability</u>**
> *Visit **mometrix.com/academy** and enter **Code: 212374***

Terms frequently used in probability:
Event – a situation that produces results of some sort (a coin toss)

Compound event – event that involves two or more items (rolling a pair of dice; taking the sum)

Outcome – a possible result in an experiment or event (heads, tails)

Desired outcome (or success) – an outcome that meets a particular set of criteria (a roll of 1 or 2 if we are looking for numbers less than 3)

Independent events – two or more events whose outcomes do not affect one another (two coins tossed at the same time)

Dependent events – two or more events whose outcomes affect one another (two cards drawn consecutively from the same deck)

Certain outcome – probability of outcome is 100% or 1

Impossible outcome – probability of outcome is 0% or 0

Mutually exclusive outcomes – two or more outcomes whose criteria cannot all be satisfied in a single outcome (a coin coming up heads and tails on the same toss)

Theoretical probability is the likelihood of a certain outcome occurring for a given event. It can be determined without actually performing the event. It is calculated as P (probability of success) = (desired outcomes)/(total outcomes).
Example:
There are 20 marbles in a bag and 5 are red. The theoretical probability of randomly selecting a red marble is 5 out of 20, (5/20 = 1/4, 0.25, or 25%).

Most of the time, when we talk about probability, we mean theoretical probability. Experimental probability, or relative frequency, is the number of times an outcome occurs in a particular experiment or a certain number of observed events.

While theoretical probability is based on what *should* happen, experimental probability is based on what *has* happened. Experimental probability is calculated in the same way as theoretical, except that actual outcomes are used instead of possible outcomes.

Theoretical and experimental probability do not always line up with one another. Theoretical probability says that out of 20 coin tosses, 10 should be heads. However, if we were actually to toss 20 coins, we might record just 5 heads. This doesn't mean that our theoretical probability is incorrect; it just means that this particular experiment had results that were different from what was predicted.

> ➤ **Review Video: <u>Theoretical and Experimental Probability</u>**
> *Visit **mometrix.com/academy** and enter **Code: 444349***

Expected Value

Expected value is a method of determining expected outcome in a random situation. It is really a sum of the weighted probabilities of the possible outcomes. Multiply the probability of an event occurring by the weight assigned to that probability (such as the amount of money won or lost). A practical application of the expected value is to determine whether a game of chance is really fair. If the sum of the weighted probabilities is greater than or equal to zero, the game is generally considered fair because the player has a fair chance to win, or at least to break even. If the expected value is less than one, then players lose more than they win. For example, a lottery drawing allows the player to choose any three-digit number, 000–999. The probability of choosing the winning number is 1:1000. If it costs $1 to play, and a winning number receives $500, the expected value is $\left(-\$1 \cdot \frac{999}{1,000}\right) +$ $\left(\$500 \cdot \frac{1}{1,000}\right) = -0.499$ or $-\$0.50$. You can expect to lose on average 50 cents for every dollar you spend.

Common Charts and Graphs

Charts and *Tables* are ways of organizing information into separate rows and columns. These rows and columns are labeled to find and to explain the information in them. Some charts and tables are organized horizontally with rows giving the details about the labeled information. Other charts and tables are organized vertically with columns giving the details about the labeled information.

Frequency Tables show how many times each value comes up within the set. A *Relative Frequency Table* shows the proportions of each value compared to the entire set. Relative frequencies are given as percents. However, the total percent for a relative frequency table may not equal 100 percent because of rounding.

This is an example of a frequency table with relative frequencies:

Favorite Color	Frequency	Relative Frequency
Blue	4	13%
Red	7	22%
Purple	3	9%
Green	6	19%
Cyan	12	38%

A *Bar Graph* is one of the few graphs that can be drawn correctly in two ways: horizontally and vertically. A bar graph is similar to a line plot because of how the data is organized on the graph. Both axes must have their categories defined for the graph to be useful. A thick line is drawn from zero to the exact value of the data. This line can be used for a number, a percentage, or other numerical value. Longer bar lengths point to greater data values. To understand a bar graph, read the labels for the axes to know the units being reported. Then look where the bars end and match this to the scale on the other axis. This will show you the connection between the axes. This bar graph shows the responses from a survey about the favorite colors of a group.

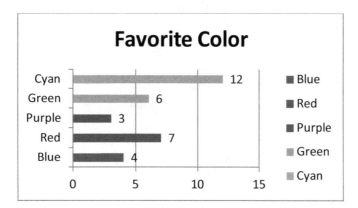

Line Graphs have one or more lines of different styles (e.g., solid or broken). These lines show the different values for a data set. Each point on the graph is shown as an ordered pair. This is similar to a Cartesian plane. In this case, the *x*- and *y*- axes are given certain units (e.g., dollars or time). Each point that is for one measurement is joined by line segments. Then, these lines show what the values are doing.

The lines may be increasing (i.e., line sloping upward), decreasing (i.e., line sloping downward), or staying the same (i.e., horizontal line). More than one set of data can be put on the same line graph. This is done to compare more than one piece of data. An example of this would be graphing test scores for different groups of students over the same stretch of time. This allows you to see which group had the greatest increase or decrease in performance over a certain amount of years. This example is shown in the graph below.

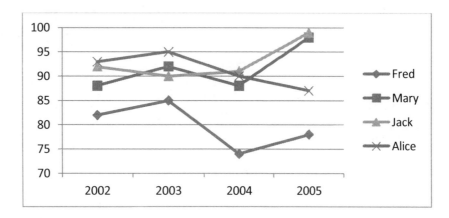

A *Line Plot*, or a *Dot Plot*, has plotted points that are NOT connected by line segments. In this graph, the horizontal axis lists the different possible values for the data. The vertical axis lists how many times one value happens. A single dot is graphed for each value. The dots in a line plot are connected. If the dots are connected, then this will not correctly represent the data.

The *5-Number Summary* of a set of data gives a very informative picture of the set. The five numbers in the summary are the minimum value, maximum value, and the three quartiles. This information gives you the range and the median of the set. Also, this information hints at how the data is spread across the median.

A *Box-and-Whiskers Plot* shows the 5-number summary on a graph. To draw a box-and-whiskers plot, place the points of the 5-number summary on a number line. Draw a box whose ends come through the points for the first and third quartiles. This is called the interquartile range. Draw a vertical line in the box that comes through the median and divides the box in half. Then, draw a line segment from the first quartile point to the minimum value. Also, draw a point from the third quartile point to the maximum value.

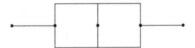

A *Pictograph* is a graph that is given in the horizontal format. This graph uses pictures or symbols to show the data. Each pictograph must have a key that defines the picture or symbol. Also, this key should give the number that stands for each picture or symbol. The pictures or symbols on a pictograph are not always shown as whole elements.

In this case, the fraction of the picture or symbol stands for the same fraction of the quantity that a whole picture or symbol represents. For example, there is a row in the pictograph with $3\frac{1}{2}$ ears of corn. Each ear of corn represents 100 stalks of corn in a field. So, this would equal $3\frac{1}{2} \times 100 = 350$ stalks of corn in the field.

Circle Graphs, or *Pie Charts*, show the relationship of each type of data compared to the whole set of data. The circle graph is divided into sections by drawing radii (i.e., plural for radius) to make central angles. These angles stand for a percentage of the circle. Each 1% of data is equal to 3.6° in the graph. So, data that stands for a 90° section of the circle graph makes up 25% of the whole. The pie chart below shows the data from the frequency table where people were asked about their favorite color.

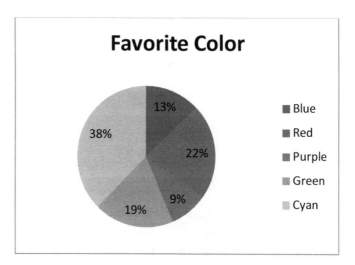

At first glance, a *Histogram* looks like a vertical bar graph. The difference is that a bar graph has a separate bar for each piece of data. A histogram has one bar for each stretch of data. For example, a histogram may have one bar for the stretch of 0–9 and one bar for the stretch of 10–19. A bar graph has numerical values on one axis.

A histogram has numbers on both axes. Each range is of equal size, and they are ordered left to right from lowest to highest. The height of each column on a histogram stands for the number of data values within that range. Like a stem and leaf plot, a histogram makes it easy to look at the graph and find which range has the greatest number of values. Below is an example of a histogram.

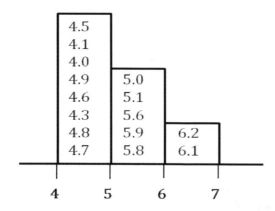

A *Stem and Leaf Plot* can outline groups of data that fall into a range of values. Each piece of data is split into two parts: the first, or left, part is called the stem. The second, or right, part is called the leaf. Each stem is listed in a column from smallest to largest. Each leaf that has the common stem is listed in that stem's row from smallest to largest.

For example, in a set of two-digit numbers, the digit in the tens place is the stem. So, the digit in the ones place is the leaf. With a stem and leaf plot, you can see which subset of numbers (10s, 20s, 30s, etc.) is the largest. This information can be found by looking at a histogram. However, a stem and leaf plot also lets you look closer and see which values fall in that range. Using all of the test scores from the line graph, we can put together a stem and leaf plot:

Test Scores								
7	4	8						
8	2	5	7	8	8			
9	0	0	1	2	2	3	5	8	9

Again, a stem-and-leaf plot is similar to histograms and frequency plots. However, a stem-and-leaf plot keeps all of the original data. In this example, you can see that almost half of the students scored in the 80s. Also, all of the data has been maintained. These plots can be used for larger numbers as well. However, they work better for small sets of data.

Bivariate Data is data from two different variables. The prefix *bi-* means *two*. In a *Scatter Plot*, each value in the set of data is put on a grid. This is similar to the Cartesian plane where each axis represents one of the two variables. When you look at the pattern made by the points on the grid, you may know if there is a relationship between the two variables. Also, you may know what that relationship is and if it exists.

The variables may be directly proportionate, inversely proportionate, or show no proportion. Also, you may be able to see if the data is linear. If the data is linear, you can find an equation to show the two variables. The following scatter plot shows the relationship between preference for brand "A" and the age of the consumers surveyed.

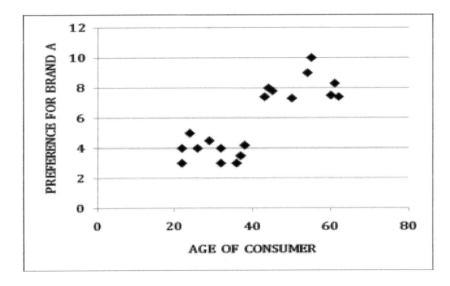

Scatter Plots are useful for knowing the types of functions that are given with the data. Also, they are helpful for finding the simple regression. A simple regression is a regression that uses an independent variable.

A regression is a chart that is used to predict future events. Linear scatter plots may be positive or negative. Many nonlinear scatter plots are exponential or quadratic. Below are some common types of scatter plots:

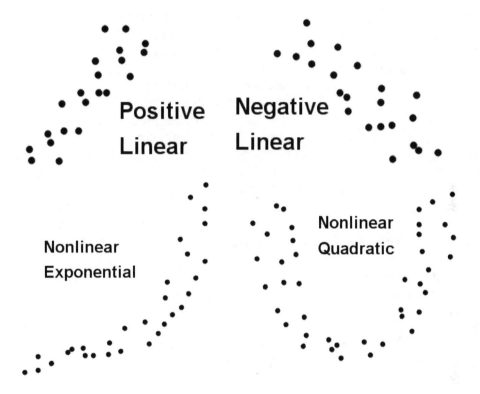

Reading Comprehension

Reading and Reasoning

Types of Passages

A **narrative** passage is a story that can be fiction or nonfiction. However, there are a few elements that a text must have in order to be classified as a narrative. First, the text must have a plot (i.e., a series of events). Narratives often proceed in a clear sequence, but this is not a requirement. If the narrative is good, then these events will be interesting to readers. Second, a narrative has characters. These characters could be people, animals, or even inanimate objects--so long as they participate in the plot. Third, a narrative passage often contains figurative language which is meant to stimulate the imagination of readers by making comparisons and observations. For instance, a metaphor, a common piece of figurative language, is a description of one thing in terms of another. *The moon was a frosty snowball* is an example of a metaphor. In the literal sense this is obviously untrue, but the comparison suggests a certain mood for the reader.

> ➤ **Review Video: Narratives**
> *Visit **mometrix.com/academy** and enter **Code: 280100***

An **expository** passage aims to inform and enlighten readers. The passage is nonfiction and usually centers around a simple, easily defined topic. Since the goal of exposition is to teach, such a passage should be as clear as possible. Often, an expository passage contains helpful organizing words, like *first*, *next*, *for example*, and *therefore*. These words keep the reader oriented in the text. Although expository passages do not need to feature colorful language and artful writing, they are often more effective with these features.

For a reader, the challenge of expository passages is to maintain steady attention. Expository passages are not always about subjects that will naturally interest a reader, and the writer is often more concerned with clarity and comprehensibility than with engaging the reader. By reading actively, you will ensure a good habit of focus when reading an expository passage.

> ➤ **Review Video: Expository Passages**
> *Visit **mometrix.com/academy** and enter **Code: 256515***

A **technical** passage is written to describe a complex object or process. Technical writing is common in medical and technological fields, in which complex ideas of mathematics, science, and engineering need to be explained simply and clearly. To ease comprehension, a technical passage usually proceeds in a very logical order. Technical passages often have clear headings and subheadings, which are used to keep the reader oriented in the text. Additionally, you will find that these passages divide sections up with numbers or letters. Many technical passages look more like an outline than a piece of prose. The amount of jargon or difficult vocabulary will vary in a technical passage depending on the intended audience. As much as possible, technical passages try to avoid language that the reader will have to research in order to understand the message, yet readers will find that jargon cannot always be avoided.

> ➤ **Review Video: <u>A Technical Passage</u>**
> *Visit **mometrix.com/academy** and enter **Code: 478923***

A **persuasive** passage is meant to change the mind of readers and lead them into agreement with the author. The persuasive intent may be very obvious or quite difficult to discern. In some cases, a persuasive passage will be indistinguishable from one that is informative. Both passages make an assertion and offer supporting details. However, a persuasive passage is more likely to appeal to the reader's emotions and to make claims based on opinion. Persuasive passages may not describe alternate positions, but--when they do--they often display significant bias. Readers may find that a persuasive passage is giving the author's viewpoint, or the passage may adopt a seemingly objective tone. A persuasive passage is successful if it can make a convincing argument and win the trust of the reader.

> ➤ **Review Video: <u>Persuasive Text and Bias</u>**
> *Visit **mometrix.com/academy** and enter **Code: 479856***

Persuasive passages tend to focus on one central argument while making many smaller claims along the way. These smaller claims are subordinate arguments that readers must accept if they are going to agree with the central argument. Thus, the central argument will only be as strong as the subordinate claims. These claims should be rooted in fact and observation, rather than subjective judgment. The best persuasive essays provide enough supporting detail to justify claims without overwhelming readers. Remember that a fact must be susceptible to independent verification (i.e., the fact must be something that readers could confirm). Also, statistics are only effective when they take into account possible objections. For instance, a statistic on the number of foreclosed houses would only be useful if it was taken over a defined interval and in a defined area. Most readers are wary of statistics because they can be misleading. The writers of your test are aware that their work will be met by inquiring readers, and your ability to maintain doubt with persuasive passages will be a benefit in your exam.

> ➤ **Review Video: <u>Persuasive Essay</u>**
> *Visit **mometrix.com/academy** and enter **Code: 621428***

Opinions are formed by emotion as well as reason, and persuasive writers often appeal to the feelings of readers. Although readers should always be skeptical of this technique, these appeals are often used in a proper and ethical manner. For instance, there are many subjects that have an obvious emotional component and therefore cannot be completely treated without an appeal to the emotions. Consider an article on drunk driving: specific examples that will alarm or sadden readers are likely to be included as an appeal to emotions. After all, drunk driving can have serious and tragic consequences. On the other hand, emotional appeals are not appropriate when they attempt to mislead readers. For instance, in political advertisements, one will observe the emphasis on the patriotism of the preferred candidate because this will encourage the audience to link their own positive feelings about the country with their opinion of the candidate. However, these advertisements often imply that the other candidate is unpatriotic which--in most cases--is far from the truth. Another common and improper emotional appeal is the use of loaded language. Referring to an avidly religious person as a "fanatic" or a passionate environmentalist as a "tree hugger" are examples of this. These terms introduce an emotional component that detracts from the argument.

> ➤ **Review Video: <u>Appeal to the Reader's Emotions</u>**
> *Visit **mometrix.com/academy** and enter **Code: 163442***

Organization of the Text

The way a text is organized can help readers to understand the author's intent and his or her conclusions. There are various ways to organize a text, and each one has a purpose and use.

Some nonfiction texts are organized to **present a problem** followed by a solution. For this type of text, the problem is often explained before the solution is offered. In some cases, as when the problem is well known, the solution may be introduced briefly at the beginning. Other passages may focus on the solution, and the problem will be referenced only occasionally. Some texts will outline multiple solutions to a problem, leaving readers to choose among them. If the author has an interest or an allegiance to one solution, he or she may fail to mention or describe accurately some of the other solutions. Readers should be careful of the author's agenda when reading a problem-solution text. Only by understanding the author's perspective and interests can one develop a proper judgment of the proposed solution.

Occasionally, authors will organize information logically in a passage so the reader can follow and locate the information within the text. Since this is not always the case with passages in an exam, you need to be familiar with other examples of provided information. Two common organizational structures are cause and effect and chronological order. When using **chronological order**, the author presents information in the order that it happened. For example, biographies are written in chronological order. The subject's birth and childhood are presented first, followed by their adult life, and lastly by the events leading up to the person's death.

In **cause and effect**, an author presents one thing that makes something else happen. For example, if one were to go to bed very late and awake very early, then they would be tired in the morning. The cause is lack of sleep, with the effect of being tired the next day.

Identifying the cause-and-effect relationships in a text can be tricky, but there are a few ways to approach this task. Often, these relationships are signaled with certain terms. When an author uses words like *because, since, in order*, and *so*, he or she is likely describing a cause-and-effect relationship. Consider the sentence: *He called her because he needed the homework.* This is a simple causal relationship in which the cause was his need for the homework, and the effect was his phone call. Yet, not all cause-and-effect relationships are marked in this way. Consider the sentences: *He called her. He needed the homework.* When the cause-and-effect relationship is not indicated with a keyword, the relationship can be discovered by asking why something happened. He called her: why? The answer is in the next sentence: He needed the homework.

Persuasive essays, in which an author tries to make a convincing argument and change the minds of readers, usually include cause-and-effect relationships. However, these relationships should not always be taken at face value. Frequently, an author will assume a cause or take an effect for granted. To read a persuasive essay effectively, readers need to judge the cause-and-effect relationships that the author is presenting. For instance, imagine an author wrote the following: *The parking deck has been unprofitable because people would prefer to ride their bikes.* The relationship is clear: the cause is that people prefer to ride their bikes, and the effect is that the parking deck has been unprofitable. However, readers should consider whether this argument is conclusive. Perhaps there are other reasons for the failure of the parking deck: a down economy, excessive fees, etc. Too often, authors present causal relationships as if they are fact rather than opinion. Readers should be on the alert for these dubious claims.

Many texts follow the **compare-and-contrast** model in which the similarities and differences between two ideas or things are explored. Analysis of the similarities between ideas is called comparison. In an ideal comparison, the author places ideas or things in an equivalent structure (i.e., the author presents the ideas in the same way). If an author wants to show the similarities between cricket and baseball, then he or she may do so by summarizing the equipment and rules for each game. Be mindful of the similarities as they appear in the passage and take note of any differences that are mentioned. Often, these small differences will only reinforce the more general similarity.

Thinking critically about ideas and conclusions can seem like a daunting task. One way to ease this task is to understand the basic elements of ideas and writing techniques. Looking at the way different ideas relate to each other can be a good way for readers to begin their analysis. For instance, sometimes authors will write about two ideas that are in opposition to each other. Or one author will provide his or her ideas on a topic, and another author may respond in opposition. The analysis of these opposing ideas is known as **contrast**. Contrast is often marred by the author's obvious partiality to one of the ideas. A discerning reader will be put off by an author who does not engage in a fair fight. In an analysis of opposing ideas, both ideas should be presented in clear and reasonable terms. If the author does prefer a side, you need to read carefully to determine the areas where the author shows or avoids this preference. In an analysis of opposing ideas, you should proceed through the passage by marking the major differences point by point with an eye that is looking for an explanation of each side's view. For instance, in an analysis of capitalism and communism, there is an importance in outlining each side's view on labor, markets, prices, personal responsibility, etc. Additionally, as you read through the passages, you should note whether the opposing views present each side in a similar manner.

Purposes for Writing

In order to be an effective reader, one must pay attention to the author's **position** and purpose. Even those texts that seem objective and impartial, like textbooks, have a position and bias. Readers need to take these positions into account when considering the author's message. When an author uses emotional language or clearly favors one side of an argument, his or her position is clear. However, the author's position may be evident not only in what he or she writes, but also in what he or she doesn't write. In a normal setting, a reader would want to review some other texts on the same topic in order to develop a view of the author's position. If this was not possible, then you would want to acquire some background about the author. However, since you are in the middle of an exam and the only source of information is the text, you should look for language and argumentation that seems to indicate a particular stance on the subject.

> **Review Video: <u>Author's Position</u>**
> *Visit **mometrix.com/academy** and enter **Code: 827954***

Usually, identifying the **purpose** of an author is easier than identifying his or her position. In most cases, the author has no interest in hiding his or her purpose. A text that is meant to entertain, for instance, should be written to please the reader. Most narratives, or stories, are written to entertain, though they may also inform or persuade. Informative texts are easy to identify, while the most difficult purpose of a text to identify is persuasion because the author has an interest in making this purpose hard to detect. When a reader discovers that the author is trying to persuade, he or she should be skeptical of the argument. For this reason persuasive texts often try to establish an entertaining tone and hope to amuse the reader into agreement. On the other hand, an informative tone may be implemented to create an appearance of authority and objectivity.

An author's purpose is evident often in the organization of the text (e.g., section headings in bold font points to an informative text). However, you may not have such organization available to you in your exam. Instead, if the author makes his or her main idea clear from the beginning, then the likely purpose of the text is to inform. If the author begins by making a claim and provides various arguments to support that claim, then the purpose is probably to persuade. If the author tells a story or seems to want the attention of the reader more than to push a particular point or deliver information, then his or her purpose is most likely to entertain. As a reader, you must judge authors on how well they accomplish their purpose. In other words, you need to consider the type of passage (e.g., technical, persuasive, etc.) that the author has written and if the author has followed the requirements of the passage type.

> **Review Video: <u>Purpose of an Author</u>**
> *Visit **mometrix.com/academy** and enter **Code: 497555***

The author's purpose for writing will affect his or her writing style and the response of the reader. In a **persuasive essay**, the author is attempting to change the reader's mind or convince him or her of something that he or she did not believe previously. There are several identifying characteristics of persuasive writing. One is opinion presented as fact. When authors attempt to persuade readers, they often present their opinions as if they were fact. Readers must be on guard for statements that sound factual but which cannot be subjected to research, observation, or experiment. Another characteristic of persuasive writing is emotional language. An author will often try to play on the emotions of readers by appealing to their sympathy or sense of morality. When an author uses colorful or evocative language with the intent of arousing the reader's passions, then the author may be attempting to persuade. Finally, in many cases, a persuasive text will give an unfair explanation of opposing positions, if these positions are mentioned at all.

An informative text is written to educate and enlighten readers. Informative texts are almost always nonfiction and are rarely structured as a story. The intention of an informative text is to deliver information in the most comprehensible way. So, look for the structure of the text to be very clear. In an informative text, the thesis statement is one--or two--sentence(s) that normally appears at the end of the first paragraph. The author may use some colorful language, but he or she is likely to put more emphasis on clarity and precision. Informative essays do not typically appeal to the emotions. They often contain facts and figures and rarely include the opinion of the author; however, readers should remain aware of the possibility for a bias as those facts are presented. Sometimes a persuasive essay can resemble an informative essay, especially if the author maintains an even tone and presents his or her views as if they were established fact.

The success or failure of an author's intent to **entertain** is determined by those who read the author's work. Entertaining texts may be either fiction or nonfiction, and they may describe real or imagined people, places, and events. Entertaining texts are often narratives or poems. A text that is written to entertain is likely to contain colorful language that engages the imagination and the emotions. Such writing often features a great deal of figurative language, which typically enlivens the subject matter with images and analogies.

Though an entertaining text is not usually written to persuade or inform, authors may accomplish both of these tasks in their work. An entertaining text may appeal to the reader's emotions and cause him or her to think differently about a particular subject. In any case, entertaining texts tend to showcase the personality of the author more than other types of writing.

When an author intends to **express feelings,** he or she may use expressive and bold language. An author may write with emotion for any number of reasons. Sometimes, authors will express feelings because they are describing a personal situation of great pain or happiness. In other situations, authors will attempt to persuade the reader and will use emotion to stir up the passions. This kind of expression is easy to identify when the writer uses phrases like *I felt* and *I sense*. However, readers may find that the author will simply describe feelings without introducing them. As a reader, you must know the importance of recognizing when an author is expressing emotion and not to become overwhelmed by sympathy or passion. Readers should maintain some detachment so that they can still evaluate the strength of the author's argument or the quality of the writing.

In a sense, almost all writing is descriptive, insofar as an author seeks to describe events, ideas, or people to the reader. Some texts, however, are primarily concerned with **description**. A descriptive text focuses on a particular subject and attempts to depict the subject in a way that will be clear to readers. Descriptive texts contain many adjectives and adverbs (i.e., words that give shades of meaning and create a more detailed mental picture for the reader). A descriptive text fails when it is unclear to the reader. A descriptive text will certainly be informative, and the passage may be persuasive and entertaining as well.

Writing Devices

Authors will use different stylistic and writing devices to make their meaning clear for readers. One of those devices is comparison and contrast. As mentioned previously, when an author describes the ways in which two things are alike, he or she is **comparing** them. When the author describes the ways in which two things are different, he or she is **contrasting** them. The "compare and contrast" essay is one of the most common forms in nonfiction. These passages are often signaled with certain words: a comparison may have indicating terms such as *both, same, like, too,* and *as well;* while a contrast may have terms like *but, however, on the other hand, instead,* and *yet.* Of course, comparisons and contrasts may be implicit without using any such signaling language. A single sentence may both compare and contrast. Consider the sentence *Brian and Sheila love ice cream, but Brian prefers vanilla and Sheila prefers strawberry*. In one sentence, the author has described both a similarity (love of ice cream) and a difference (favorite flavor).

> ➢ **Review Video: <u>Compare and Contrast</u>**
> *Visit **mometrix.com/academy** and enter **Code: 798319***

One of the most common text structures is **cause and effect**. A cause is an act or event that makes something happen, and an effect is the thing that happens as a result of the cause. A cause-and-effect relationship is not always explicit, but there are some terms in English that signal causes, such as *since*, *because*, and *due to*. Furthermore, terms that signal effects include *consequently, therefore, this lead(s) to*. As an example, consider the sentence *Because the sky was clear, Ron did not bring an umbrella*. The cause is the clear sky, and the effect is that Ron did not bring an umbrella. However, readers may find that sometimes the cause-and-effect relationship will not be clearly noted. For instance, the sentence *He was late and missed the meeting* does not contain any signaling words, but the sentence still contains a cause (he was late) and an effect (he missed the meeting).

Be aware of the possibility for a single cause to have multiple effects (e.g., *Single cause*: Because you left your homework on the table, your dog engulfs the assignment. *Multiple effects*: As a result, you receive a failing grade; your parents do not allow you to visit your friends; you miss out on the new movie and holding the hand of a potential significant other).

Also, the possibility of a single effect to have multiple causes (e.g.. *Single effect*: Alan has a fever. *Multiple causes*: An unexpected cold front came through the area, and Alan forgot to take his multi-vitamin to avoid being sick.)

Additionally, an effect can in turn be the cause of another effect, in what is known as a cause-and-effect chain. (e.g., As a result of her disdain for procrastination, Lynn prepared for her exam. This led to her passing her test with high marks. Hence, her resume was accepted and her application was approved.)

Another element that impacts a text is the author's point-of-view. The **point of view** of a text is the perspective from which a passage is told. An author will always have a point of view about a story before he or she draws up a plot line. The author will know what events they want to take place, how they want the characters to interact, and how they want the story to resolve. An author will also have an opinion on the topic or series of events which is presented in the story that is based on their prior experience and beliefs.

The two main points of view that authors use--especially in a work of fiction--are first person and third person. If the narrator of the story is also the main character, or *protagonist*, the text is written in first-person point of view. In first person, the author writes from the perspective of *I*. Third-person point of view is probably the most common that authors use in their passages. Using third person, authors refer to each character by using *he* or *she*. In third-person omniscient, the narrator is not a character in the story and tells the story of all of the characters at the same time.

> ➢ **Review Video: Point of View**
> *Visit mometrix.com/academy and enter Code:* **383336**

Transitional words and phrases are devices that guide readers through a text. You are no doubt familiar with the common transitions, though you may never have considered how they operate. Some transitional phrases (*after, before, during, in the middle of*) give information about time. Some indicate that an example is about to be given (*for example, in fact, for instance*). Writers use them to compare (*also, likewise*) and contrast (*however, but, yet*). Transitional words and phrases can suggest addition (*and, also, furthermore, moreover*) and logical relationships (*if, then, therefore, as a result, since*). Finally, transitional words and phrases can separate the steps in a process (*first, second, last*).

> ➢ **Review Video: Transitional Words and Phrases**
> *Visit mometrix.com/academy and enter Code:* **197796**

Understanding a Passage

One of the most important skills in reading comprehension is the identification of **topics** and **main ideas.** There is a subtle difference between these two features. The topic is the subject of a text (i.e., what the text is all about). The main idea, on the other hand, is the most important point being made by the author. The topic is usually expressed in a few words at the most while the main idea often needs a full sentence to be completely defined. As an example, a short passage might have the topic of penguins and the main idea could be written as *Penguins are different from other birds in many ways*. In most nonfiction writing, the topic and the main idea will be stated directly and often appear in a sentence at the very beginning or end of the text. When being tested on an understanding of the author's topic, you may be able to skim the passage for the general idea, by reading only the first sentence of each paragraph. A body paragraph's first sentence is often--but not always--the main topic sentence which gives you a summary of the content in the paragraph.

However, there are cases in which the reader must figure out an unstated topic or main idea. In these instances, you must read every sentence of the text and try to come up with an overarching idea that is supported by each of those sentences.

Note: A thesis statement should not be confused with the main idea of the passage. While the main idea gives a brief, general summary of a text, the thesis statement provides a specific perspective on an issue that the author supports with evidence.

> ➢ **Review Video: Topics and Main Ideas**
> *Visit mometrix.com/academy and enter Code:* **407801**

Supporting details provide evidence and backing for the main point. In order to show that a main idea is correct, or valid, authors add details that prove their point. All texts contain details, but they are only classified as supporting details when they serve to reinforce some larger point. Supporting details are most commonly found in informative and persuasive texts. In some cases, they will be clearly indicated with terms like *for example* or *for instance*, or they will be enumerated with terms like *first*, *second*, and *last*. However, you need to be prepared for texts that do not contain those indicators. As a reader, you should consider whether the author's supporting details really back up his or her main point. Supporting details can be factual and correct, yet they may not be relevant to the author's point. Conversely, supporting details can seem pertinent, but they can be ineffective because they are based on opinion or assertions that cannot be proven.

> ➤ **Review Video: <u>Supporting Details</u>**
> *Visit **mometrix.com/academy** and enter **Code: 396297***

An example of a main idea is: *Giraffes live in the Serengeti of Africa.* A supporting detail about giraffes could be: *A giraffe in this region benefits from a long neck by reaching twigs and leaves on tall trees.* The main idea gives the general idea that the text is about giraffes. The supporting detail gives a specific fact about how the giraffes eat.

As opposed to a main idea, themes are seldom expressed directly in a text and can be difficult to identify. A **theme** is an issue, an idea, or a question raised by the text. For instance, a theme of *Cinderella* (the Charles Perrault version) is perseverance as the title character serves her step-sisters and step-mother, and the prince seeks to find the girl with the missing slipper. A passage may have many themes, and you--as a dedicated reader-- must take care to identify only themes that you are asked to find. One common characteristic of themes is that they raise more questions than they answer. In a good piece of fiction, authors are trying to elevate the reader's perspective and encourage him or her to consider the themes in a deeper way. In the process of reading, one can identify themes by constantly asking about the general issues that the text is addressing. A good way to evaluate an author's approach to a theme is to begin reading with a question in mind (e.g., How does this text approach the theme of love?) and to look for evidence in the text that addresses that question.

> ➤ **Review Video: <u>Theme</u>**
> *Visit **mometrix.com/academy** and enter **Code: 732074***

Evaluating a Passage

When reading informational texts, there is importance in understanding the logical conclusion of the author's ideas. **Identifying a logical conclusion** can help you determine whether you agree with the writer or not. Coming to this conclusion is much like making an inference: the approach requires you to combine the information given by the text with what you already know in order to make a logical conclusion. If the author intended the reader to draw a certain conclusion, then you can expect the author's argumentation and detail to be leading in that direction.

One way to approach the task of drawing conclusions is to make brief notes of all the points made by the author. When the notes are arranged on paper, they may clarify the logical conclusion. Another way to approach conclusions is to consider whether the reasoning of the author raises any pertinent questions. Sometimes you will be able to draw several conclusions from a passage. On occasion these will be conclusions that were never imagined by the author. Therefore, be aware that these conclusions must be supported directly by the text.

> ➢ **Review Video: Identifying a Logical Conclusion**
> *Visit **mometrix.com/academy** and enter **Code: 281653***

The term **text evidence** refers to information that supports a main point or minor points and can help lead the reader to a conclusion. Information used as text evidence is precise, descriptive, and factual. A main point is often followed by supporting details that provide evidence to back-up a claim. For example, a passage may include the claim that winter occurs during opposite months in the Northern and Southern hemispheres. Text evidence based on this claim may include countries where winter occurs in opposite months along with reasons that winter occurs at different times of the year in separate hemispheres (due to the tilt of the Earth as it rotates around the sun).

> ➢ **Review Video: Text Evidence**
> *Visit **mometrix.com/academy** and enter **Code: 486236***

The text used to support an argument can be the argument's downfall if the text is not credible. A text is **credible**, or believable, when the author is knowledgeable and objective, or unbiased. The author's motivations for writing the text play a critical role in determining the credibility of the text and must be evaluated when assessing that credibility. Reports written about the ozone layer by an environmental scientist and a hairdresser will have a different level of credibility.

A reader should always be drawing conclusions from the text. Sometimes conclusions are implied from written information, and other times the information is **stated directly** within the passage. One should always aim to draw conclusions from information stated within a passage, rather than to draw them from mere implications. At times an author may provide some information and then describe a counterargument. Readers should be alert for direct statements that are subsequently rejected or weakened by the author. Furthermore, you should always read through the entire passage before drawing conclusions. Many readers are trained to expect the author's conclusions at either the beginning or the end of the passage, but many texts do not adhere to this format.

Drawing conclusions from information implied within a passage requires confidence on the part of the reader. **Implications** are things that the author does not state directly, but readers can assume based on what the author does say. Consider the following passage: *I stepped outside and opened my umbrella. By the time I got to work, the cuffs of my pants were soaked.* The author never states that it is raining, but this fact is clearly implied. Conclusions based on implication must be well supported by the text. In order to draw a solid conclusion, readers should have multiple pieces of evidence. If readers have only one piece, they must be assured that there is no other possible explanation than their conclusion. A good reader will be able to draw many conclusions from information implied by the text which will be a great help in the exam.

As an aid to drawing conclusions, **outlining** the information contained in the passage should be a familiar skill to readers. An effective outline will reveal the structure of the passage and will lead to solid conclusions. An effective outline will have a title that refers to the basic subject of the text though the title needs not recapitulate the main idea. In most outlines, the main idea will be the first major section. Each major idea of the passage will be established as the head of a category. For instance, the most common outline format calls for the main ideas of the passage to be indicated with Roman numerals. In an effective outline of this kind, each of the main ideas will be represented by a Roman numeral and none of the Roman numerals will designate minor details or secondary ideas. Moreover, all supporting ideas and details should be placed in the appropriate place on the outline. An outline does not need to include every detail listed in the text, but the outline should feature all of those that are central to the argument or message. Each of these details should be listed under the appropriate main idea.

Ideas from a text can also be organized using **graphic organizers**. A graphic organizer is a way to simplify information and take key points from the text. A graphic organizer such as a timeline may have an event listed for a corresponding date on the timeline while an outline may have an event listed under a key point that occurs in the text. Each reader needs to create the type of graphic organizer that works the best for him or her in terms of being able to recall information from a story. Examples include a *spider-map,* which takes a main idea from the story and places it in a bubble with supporting points branching off the main idea. An *outline* is useful for diagramming the main and supporting points of the entire story, and a *Venn diagram* classifies information as separate or overlapping.

> ➤ **Review Video:** <u>Graphic Organizers</u>
> *Visit **mometrix.com/academy** and enter **Code: 665513***

A helpful tool is the ability to **summarize** the information that you have read in a paragraph or passage format. This process is similar to creating an effective outline. First, a summary should accurately define the main idea of the passage though the summary does not need to explain this main idea in exhaustive detail. The summary should continue by laying out the most important supporting details or arguments from the passage. All of the significant supporting details should be included, and none of the details included should be irrelevant or insignificant. Also, the summary should accurately report all of these details. Too often, the desire for brevity in a summary leads to the sacrifice of clarity or accuracy. Summaries are often difficult to read because they omit all of the graceful language, digressions, and asides that distinguish great writing. However, an effective summary should contain much the same message as the original text.

Paraphrasing is another method that the reader can use to aid in comprehension. When paraphrasing, one puts what they have read into their words by rephrasing what the author has written, or one "translates" all of what the author shared into their words by including as many details as they can.

Responding to a Passage

When reading a good passage, readers are moved to engage actively in the text. One part of being an active reader involves making predictions. A **prediction** is a guess about what will happen next. Readers constantly make predictions based on what they have read and what they already know. Consider the following sentence: *Staring at the computer screen in shock, Kim blindly reached over for the brimming glass of water on the shelf to her side.* The sentence suggests that Kim is agitated, and that she is not looking at the glass that she is going to pick up. So, a reader might predict that Kim is going to knock over the glass. Of course, not every prediction will be accurate: perhaps Kim will pick the glass up cleanly. Nevertheless, the author has certainly created the expectation that the water might be spilled. Predictions are always subject to revision as the reader acquires more information.

> **Review Video: <u>Predictions</u>**
> Visit *mometrix.com/academy* and enter **Code: 437248**

Test-taking tip: To respond to questions requiring future predictions, your answers should be based on evidence of past or present behavior.

Readers are often required to understand a text that claims and suggests ideas without stating them directly. An **inference** is a piece of information that is implied but not written outright by the author. For instance, consider the following sentence: *After the final out of the inning, the fans were filled with joy and rushed the field*. From this sentence, a reader can infer that the fans were watching a baseball game and their team won the game. Readers should take great care to avoid using information beyond the provided passage before making inferences. As you practice with drawing inferences, you will find that they require concentration and attention.

> **Review Video: <u>Inference</u>**
> Visit *mometrix.com/academy* and enter **Code: 379203**

Test-taking tip: While being tested on your ability to make correct inferences, you must look for contextual clues. An answer can be *true* but not *correct*. The contextual clues will help you find the answer that is the best answer out of the given choices. Be careful in your reading to understand the context in which a phrase is stated. When asked for the implied meaning of a statement made in the passage, you should immediately locate the statement and read the context in which the statement was made. Also, look for an answer choice that has a similar phrase to the statement in question.

Readers must be able to identify a text's **sequence**, or the order in which things happen. Often, when the sequence is very important to the author, the text is indicated with signal words like *first*, *then*, *next*, and *last*. However, a sequence can be merely implied and must be noted by the reader. Consider the sentence *He walked through the garden and gave water and fertilizer to the plants*. Clearly, the man did not walk through the garden before he collected water and fertilizer for the plants. So, the implied sequence is that he first collected water, then he collected fertilizer, next he walked through the garden, and last he gave water or fertilizer as necessary to the plants. Texts do not always proceed in an orderly sequence from first to last. Sometimes they begin at the end and start over at the beginning. As a reader, you can enhance your understanding of the passage by taking brief notes to clarify the sequence.

In addition to inference and prediction, readers must often **draw conclusions** about the information they have read. When asked for a *conclusion* that may be drawn, look for critical "hedge" phrases, such as *likely*, *may*, *can*, *will often*, among many others. When you are being tested on this knowledge, remember the question that writers insert into these hedge phrases to cover every possibility. Often an answer will be wrong simply because there is no room for exception. Extreme positive or negative answers (such as always or never) are usually not correct. The reader <u>should not</u> use any outside knowledge that is not gathered from the passage to answer the related questions. Correct answers can be derived straight from the passage.

Building a Vocabulary

The **denotative** meaning of a word is the literal meaning. The **connotative** meaning goes beyond the denotative meaning to include the emotional reaction that a word may invoke. The connotative meaning often takes the denotative meaning a step further due to associations which the reader makes with the denotative meaning. Readers can differentiate between the denotative and connotative meanings by first recognizing how authors use each meaning. Most non-fiction, for example, is fact-based and authors do not use flowery, figurative language. The reader can assume that the writer is using the denotative meaning of words. In fiction, the author may use the connotative meaning. Readers can determine whether the author is using the denotative or connotative meaning of a word by implementing context clues.

> ➢ **Review Video: <u>Denotative and Connotative Meanings</u>**
> *Visit **mometrix.com/academy** and enter **Code: 736707***

Readers of all levels will encounter words that they have either never seen or encountered on a limited basis. The best way to define a word in **context** is to look for nearby words that can assist in learning the meaning of the word. For instance, unfamiliar nouns are often accompanied by examples that provide a definition. Consider the following sentence: *Dave arrived at the party in hilarious garb: a leopard-print shirt, buckskin trousers, and high heels.* If a reader was unfamiliar with the meaning of garb, he or she could read the examples (i.e., a leopard-print shirt, buckskin trousers, and high heels) and quickly determine that the word means *clothing*. Examples will not always be this obvious. Consider this sentence: *Parsley, lemon, and flowers were just a few of items he used as garnishes.* Here, the word *garnishes* is exemplified by parsley, lemon, and flowers. Readers who have eaten in a few restaurants will probably be able to identify a garnish as something used to decorate a plate.

> ➢ **Review Video: <u>Context</u>**
> *Visit **mometrix.com/academy** and enter **Code: 613660***

In addition to looking at the context of a passage, readers can use contrasts to define an unfamiliar word in context. In many sentences, the author will not describe the unfamiliar word directly; instead, he or she will describe the opposite of the unfamiliar word. Thus, you are provided with some information that will bring you closer to defining the word. Consider the following example: *Despite his intelligence, Hector's low brow and bad posture made him look obtuse.* The author writes that Hector's appearance does not convey intelligence. Therefore, *obtuse* must mean unintelligent. Here is another example: *Despite the horrible weather, we were beatific about our trip to Alaska.* The word *despite* indicates that the speaker's feelings were at odds with the weather. Since the weather is described as *horrible*, then *beatific* must mean something positive.

In some cases, there will be very few contextual clues to help a reader define the meaning of an unfamiliar word. When this happens, one strategy that readers may employ is **substitution**. A good reader will brainstorm some possible synonyms for the given word, and he or she will substitute these words into the sentence. If the sentence and the surrounding passage continue to make sense, then the substitution has revealed at least some information about the unfamiliar word. Consider the sentence: *Frank's admonition rang in her ears as she climbed the mountain.* A reader unfamiliar with *admonition* might come up with some substitutions like *vow*, *promise*, *advice*, *complaint*, or *compliment*. All of these words make general sense of the sentence though their meanings are diverse. The process has suggested; however, that an admonition is some sort of message. The substitution strategy is rarely able to pinpoint a precise definition, but this process can be effective as a last resort.

Occasionally, you will be able to define an unfamiliar word by looking at the descriptive words in the context. Consider the following sentence: *Fred dragged the recalcitrant boy kicking and screaming up the stairs.* The words *dragged*, *kicking*, and *screaming* all suggest that the boy does not want to go up the stairs. The reader may assume that *recalcitrant* means something like unwilling or protesting. In this example, an unfamiliar adjective was identified.

Additionally, using description to define an unfamiliar noun is a common practice compared to unfamiliar adjectives, as in this sentence: *Don's wrinkled frown and constantly shaking fist identified him as a curmudgeon of the first order*. Don is described as having a *wrinkled frown and constantly shaking fist* suggesting that a *curmudgeon* must be a grumpy man. Contrasts do not always provide detailed information about the unfamiliar word, but they at least give the reader some clues.

When a word has more than one meaning, readers can have difficulty with determining how the word is being used in a given sentence. For instance, the verb *cleave*, can mean either *join* or *separate*. When readers come upon this word, they will have to select the definition that makes the most sense. Consider the following sentence: *Hermione's knife cleaved the bread cleanly*. Since, a knife cannot join bread together, the word must indicate separation. A slightly more difficult example would be the sentence: *The birds cleaved together as they flew from the oak tree.* Immediately, the presence of the word *together* should suggest that in this sentence *cleave* is being used to mean *join*. Discovering the intent of a word with multiple meanings requires the same tricks as defining an unknown word: look for contextual clues and evaluate the substituted words.

Critical Thinking Skills

Opinions, Facts, and Fallacies

Critical thinking skills are mastered through understanding various types of writing and the different purposes of authors in writing their passages. Every author writes for a purpose. When you understand their purpose and how they accomplish their goal, you will be able to analyze their writing and determine whether or not you agree with their conclusions.

Readers must always be conscious of the distinction between fact and opinion. A **fact** can be subjected to analysis and can be either proved or disproved. An **opinion**, on the other hand, is the author's personal thoughts or feelings which may not be alterable by research or evidence. If the author writes that the distance from New York to Boston is about two hundred miles, then he or she is stating a fact. If an author writes that New York is too crowded, then he or she is giving an opinion because there is no objective standard for overpopulation. An opinion may be indicated by words like *believe*, *think*, or *feel*. Readers must be aware that an opinion may be supported by facts. For instance, the author might give the population density of New York as a reason for an overcrowded population. An opinion supported by fact tends to be more convincing. On the other hand, when authors support their opinions with other opinions, readers should not be persuaded by the argument to any degree.

When you have an argumentative passage, you need to be sure that facts are presented to the reader from reliable sources. An opinion is what the author thinks about a given topic. An opinion is not common knowledge or proven by expert sources, instead the information is the personal beliefs and thoughts of the author. To distinguish between fact and opinion, a reader needs to consider the type of source that is presenting information, the information that backs-up a claim, and the author's motivation to have a certain point-of-view on a given topic. For example, if a panel of scientists has conducted multiple studies on the effectiveness of taking a certain vitamin, then the results are more likely to be factual than a company that is selling a vitamin and claims that taking the vitamin can produce positive effects. The company is motivated to sell their product, and the scientists are using the scientific method to prove a theory. Remember: if you find sentences that contain phrases such as "I think...", then the statement is an opinion.

> ➤ **Review Video: Fact or Opinion**
> *Visit mometrix.com/academy and enter Code:* **870899**

In their attempts to persuade, writers often make mistakes in their thinking patterns and writing choices. These patterns and choices are important to understand so you can make an informed decision. Every author has a point-of-view, but authors demonstrate a bias when they ignore reasonable counterarguments or distort opposing viewpoints. A bias is evident whenever the author is unfair or inaccurate in his or her presentation. Bias may be intentional or unintentional, and readers should be skeptical of the author's argument. Remember that a biased author may still be correct; however, the author will be correct in spite of his or her bias, not because of the bias.

A **stereotype** is like a bias, yet a stereotype is applied specifically to a group or place. Stereotyping is considered to be particularly abhorrent because the practice promotes negative generalizations about people. Readers should be very cautious of authors who stereotype in their writing. These faulty assumptions typically reveal the author's ignorance and lack of curiosity.

> ➢ **Review Video: <u>Bias and Stereotype</u>**
> Visit *mometrix.com/academy* and enter *Code:* **644829**

Literature

Literary Genres

The purpose of literary genres is to classify and analyze literature that separates texts into the basic generic types of poetry, drama, fiction, and nonfiction. There are numerous subdivisions within a genre, including such categories as novels, novellas, and short stories in fiction. Drama may also be divided into the main categories of comedy and tragedy. Genres can have overlap, and the distinctions among them are blurred. Examples include the *nonfiction novel* and *docudrama*, as well as many others.

Fiction is a general term for any form of literary narrative that is invented or imagined as opposed to a true event. A work of fiction on your exam will include a passage that has been written for your exam, or one that has been taken from a published work. There is a good chance that you will encounter a fictional work on your exam that you will recognize as the writers of your exam are aware of the literary canon. During your exam, if you recognize an excerpted piece from a published work, then you still need to read the text thoroughly once before going to the test questions. That applies to the other genres (i.e., poetry and drama) as well. Now, let's start with the genre of fiction.

Prose is derived from Latin and means "straightforward discourse." Prose fiction, although having many categories, may be divided into three main groups:
- **Short stories**: a fictional narrative that usually contains fewer than 20,000 words. Short stories have only a few characters and generally describe one major event or insight. The short story began in magazines in the late 1800s and has found an audience ever since.
- **Novels**: a longer work of fiction that may contain a large cast of characters and an extensive plot. The emphasis may be on an event, action, social problem, or an experience. An addition to the genre came in 1966 when Truman Capote's *In Cold Blood* was published and created the nonfiction novel category. Note: novels may be written in verse.
- **Novellas**: a work of narrative fiction that is longer than a short story but not as long as a novel. Novellas may also be called short novels or novelettes. They originated from the German tradition and have become a common form in literature throughout the world.

Many elements influence a work of prose fiction. Some important ones are:
- Speech and dialogue: Characters may speak for themselves or through the narrator. Depending on the author's aim, dialogue may be realistic or fantastic.

- Thoughts and mental processes: There may be internal dialogue used as a device for plot development or character understanding.
- Dramatic involvement: Some narrators encourage readers to become involved in the events of the story, whereas other authors attempt to distance readers through literary devices.
- Action: The information that advances the plot or involves new interactions between the characters.
- Duration: The time frame of the work may be long or short, and the relationship between described time and narrative time may vary.
- Setting and description: Is the setting critical to the plot or characters? How are the action scenes described?
- Themes: This is any perspective or topic that is given sustained attention.
- Symbolism: Authors often veil meanings through imagery and other literary constructions.

> **Review Video: Elements that Influence Fiction**
> *Visit **mometrix.com/academy** and enter **Code:** 789211*

Fiction extends beyond the realm of prose fiction. Songs, ballads, epics, and narrative poems are examples of non-prose fiction. A full definition of fiction must include not only the work itself but also the framework in which the work is read. Literary fiction includes many works of historical fiction that refer to real people, places, and events that are treated as if they were true. These imaginary elements enrich and broaden literary expression.

When analyzing fiction, you need to read slowly and carefully throughout the passage. The plot of a narrative can become so entertaining that the language of the work is ignored. The language of an author's work (i.e., the author's choice of vocabulary) should not simply be a way to relate a plot—the language should yield many insights to the judicious reader. Some prose fiction is based on the reader's engagement with the language rather than the story. A studious reader will analyze the mode of expression as well as the narrative. A reward of reading in this manner is to discover how the author uses different language to describe familiar objects, events, or emotions. Some works have the reader focus on an author's unorthodox use of language, whereas others may emphasize characters or storylines. The events of a story are not always the critical element in the work. You may find this approach to reading to be a struggle at first, but the rewards overshadow the initial difficulty.

Plot lines are one way to visualize the information given in a story. Every plot line follows the same stages. One can identify each of these stages in every story that they read. These stages include the introduction, rising action, conflict, climax, falling action, and resolution. The introduction tells readers the point of the story and sets up the plot. The rising action is the events that lead up to the conflict (e.g., a problem that arises) with the climax at the peak. The falling action is what happens after the climax of the conflict. The resolution is the conclusion and often has the final solution to the problem in the conflict. A plot line looks like this:

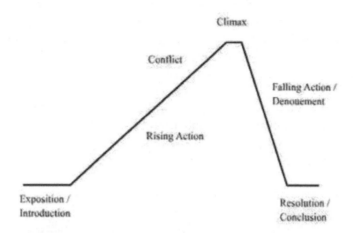

> ➢ **Review Video:** <u>Plot Lines</u>
> *Visit **mometrix.com/academy** and enter **Code:** **944011***

Most texts place events in chronological order. However, some authors may employ an unorthodox structure in order to achieve a certain effect. For instance, many of the Greek epics begin *in medias res* (i.e., in the middle of things). The text begins with an account of a climactic moment. Then, the author goes back to the beginning to describe how events led up to that climax. This technique is found in mystery novels: a crime is committed, and the detective must reconstruct the events that led to the crime. For the reader, you may want to keep in mind the cause-and-effect relationships that shape the story. By definition, a cause must precede an effect. Therefore, an outline of the various causes and effects in a text will mimic the chronological sequence. Readers should remember that the order in which events are described in a text is not necessarily the order in which they occurred.

The **narrator** is a central part of any work of fiction and can give insight about the purpose of the work and the main themes and ideas. The following are important questions to address in order to understand the voice and role of the narrator and incorporate that voice into an overall understanding of the passage:
- Who is the narrator of the passage? What is the narrator's perspective: first person or third person? What is the role of the narrator in the plot? Are there changes in narrators or the perspective of narrators?
- Does the narrator explain things in the passage or does meaning emerge from the plot and events? The personality of the narrator is important. The narrator may have a vested interest in the description of a character or an event. Some narratives follow the time sequence of the plot, whereas others do not follow the sequence. A narrator may express approval or disapproval about a character or events in the work.

- 64 -

- Tone is the attitude expressed by a character through his or her words. Who is actually being addressed by the narrator? Is the tone familiar or formal, intimate or impersonal? Does the vocabulary suggest clues about the narrator?

> ➤ **Review Video: The Narrator**
> *Visit **mometrix.com/academy** and enter **Code:** 742528*

A **character** is a person intimately involved with the plot and development of the passage. Development of the passage's characters not only moves the story along but also tells the reader about the passage itself. There is usually a physical description of the character, but this may be omitted in modern and postmodern passages as these works focus often on the psychological state or motivation of the character. The choice of a character's name may give valuable clues to his or her role in the work.

Characters can be identified as flat, round, or stock. Flat characters tend to be minor figures that may undergo some change or none at all. Round characters (those understood from a well-rounded view) are central to the story and tend to change at the unfolding of the plot. Stock characters--like flat characters--fill out the story without influencing the story.

Modern literature has been affected greatly by Freudian psychology and given rise to such devices as interior monologue and magical realism as methods of understanding characters in a work. These give readers a complex understanding of the inner lives of the characters and enrich the understanding of relationships between characters.

> ➤ **Review Video: Characters**
> *Visit **mometrix.com/academy** and enter **Code:** 429493*

Prose is ordinary spoken language as opposed to verse (i.e., language with metric patterns). The everyday, normal communication is known as prose and can be found in textbooks, memos, reports, articles, short stories, and novels. Distinguishing characteristics of prose include:
- Some sort of rhythm may be present, but there is no formal arrangement.
- The common unit of organization is the sentence which may include literary devices of repetition and balance.
- There must be coherent relationships among sentences.

Poetry, or verse, is the manipulation of language with respect to meaning, meter, sound, and rhythm. Lines of poetry vary in length and scope, and they may or may not rhyme. Related groups of lines are called stanzas and may be any length. Some poems are as short as a few lines, and some are as long as a book.

A line of poetry can be any length and can have any metrical pattern. A line is determined by the physical position of the words on a page. A line is one group of words that follows the next group in a stanza. Lines may or may not have punctuation at the end depending on the need for punctuation. Consider the following example from John Milton:
> "When I consider how my light is spent,
> E're half my days, in this dark world and wide,"

A stanza is a group of lines. The grouping denotes a relationship among the lines. A stanza can be any length, but the separation of lines into different stanzas indicates an intentional pattern created by the poet. The breaks between stanzas indicate a change of subject or thought. As a group of lines, the stanza is a melodic unit that can be analyzed for metrical patterns and rhyme patterns. Stanzas of a certain length have been named to indicate an author's purpose with a form of poetry. A few examples include the couplet (two lines), the tercet (three lines), and the quatrain (four lines).

Another important genre is **drama**: a play written to be spoken aloud. The drama is in many ways inseparable from performance. Ideally, reading drama involves using imagination to visualize and re-create the play with characters and settings. Readers stage the play in their imagination and watch characters interact and developments unfold. Sometimes this involves simulating a theatrical presentation, while other times you need to imagine the events. In either case, you are imagining the unwritten to recreate the dramatic experience. Novels present some of the same problems, but a narrator will provide much more information about the setting, characters, inner dialogues, and many other supporting details. In drama, much of this is missing, and you are required to use your powers of projection and imagination to understand the dramatic work. There are many empty spaces in dramatic texts that must be filled by the reader to appreciate the work.

> ➤ **Review Video: <u>Dramas</u>**
> *Visit **mometrix.com/academy** and enter **Code: 216060***

Figurative Language

There are many types of language devices that authors use to convey their meaning in a descriptive way. Understanding these concepts will help you understand what you read. These types of devices are called *figurative language* – language that goes beyond the literal meaning of a word or phrase. **Descriptive language** that evokes imagery in the reader's mind is one type of figurative language. **Exaggeration** is another type of figurative language. Also, when you compare two things, you are using figurative language. **Similes** and **metaphors** are ways of comparing things, and both are types of figurative language commonly found in poetry. An example of figurative language (a simile in this case): *The child howled like a coyote when her mother told her to pick up the toys*. In this example, the child's howling is compared to that of a coyote and helps the reader understand the sound being made by the child.

A **figure-of-speech**, sometimes termed a rhetorical figure or device is a word or phrase that departs from straightforward, literal language. Figures-of-speech are often used and crafted for emphasis, freshness of expression, or clarity. However, clarity of a passage may suffer from use of these devices.

As an example of the figurative use of a word, consider the sentence: *I am going to crown you.* The author may mean:
- I am going to place a literal crown on your head.
- I am going to symbolically exalt you to the place of kingship.

- I am going to punch you in the head with my clenched fist.
- I am going to put a second checker's piece on top of your checker piece to signify that it has become a king.

> **Review Video: Figure of Speech**
> *Visit mometrix.com/academy and enter Code:* **111295**

An **allusion** is a comparison of someone or something to a person or event in history or literature. Allusions that refer to people or events that are more or less contemporary are called topical allusions. Those referring to specific persons are called personal allusions. For example, *His desire for power was his Achilles' heel*. This example refers to Achilles, a notable hero in Greek mythology who was known to be invincible with the exception of his heels. Today, the term *Achilles' heel* refers to an individual's weakness.

> **Review Video: Allusion**
> *Visit mometrix.com/academy and enter Code:* **294065**

Alliteration is a stylistic device, or literary technique, in which successive words (more strictly, stressed syllables) begin with the same sound or letter. Alliteration is a frequent tool in poetry and is common in prose--particularly to highlight short phrases. Especially in poetry, alliteration contributes to the euphony (i.e., a pleasing or harmonious sound) of the passage. For instance, *We thrashed through the thick forest with our blades*. In this example, a *th* sound is somewhat difficult to make quickly in four consecutive words. Thus, the phrase conveys the difficulty of moving through tall grass. If the author is trying to suggest this difficulty, then the alliteration is a success. Now, consider the description of eyes as *glassy globes of glitter*. This is alliteration since the initial *gl* sound is used three times. However, one might question whether this awkward sound is appropriate for a description of pretty eyes. The phrase is not especially pleasant to the ear and is not a very good implementation of alliteration. Related to alliteration is *assonance*, the repetition of vowel sounds, and *consonance*, the repetition of consonant sounds. Assonance is the repetition of vowel sounds in a phrase as in: *Low and slow, he rolled the coal.* Assonance functions in much the same way as alliteration.

> **Review Video: Alliteration**
> *Visit mometrix.com/academy and enter Code:* **462837**

A **metaphor** is a type of figurative language in which the writer equates one thing with a different thing. For instance: *The bird was an arrow arcing through the sky*. In this sentence, the arrow is serving as a metaphor for the bird. The point of a metaphor is to encourage the reader to consider the item being described in a different way. Let's continue with this metaphor for a bird: you are asked to envision the bird's flight as being similar to the arc of an arrow. So, you imagine the flight to be swift and bending.

Metaphors are a way for the author to describe an item without being direct and obvious. This literary device is a lyrical and suggestive way of providing information. Note that the reference for a metaphor will not always be mentioned explicitly by the author. Consider the following description of a forest in winter: *Swaying skeletons reached for the sky and groaned as the wind blew through them*. In this example, the author is using *skeletons* as a metaphor for leafless trees. This metaphor creates a spooky tone while inspiring the reader's imagination.

> ➢ **Review Video: Metaphor**
> *Visit **mometrix.com/academy** and enter **Code: 133295***

Metonymy is referring to one thing in terms of a closely related thing. This is similar to metaphor, but there is not as much distance between the description and the thing being described. An example of metonymy is referring to the news media as *the press*, when of course *the press* is the device that prints newspapers. Metonymy is a way of referring to something without having to repeat the name constantly. **Synecdoche**, on the other hand, refers to a whole by one of the parts. An example of synecdoche would be calling a police officer a *badge*. Synecdoche, like metonymy, is an easy way of referring without having to overuse certain words. The device also allows writers to emphasize aspects of the thing being described. For instance, referring to businessmen as *suits* suggests professionalism, conformity, and blandness.

Hyperbole is overstatement for effect. For example: *He jumped ten feet in the air when he heard the good news*. Obviously, no person has the natural ability to jump ten feet in the air. The author exaggerates because the hyperbole conveys the extremity of emotion. If the author simply said: *He jumped when he heard the good news*, then readers would be led to think that the character is not experiencing an extreme emotion. Hyperbole can be dangerous if the author does not exaggerate enough. For instance, if the author wrote, *He jumped two feet in the air when he heard the good news*, then readers may assume that the author is writing a factual statement, not an exaggeration. Readers should be cautious with confusing or vague hyperboles as some test questions may have a hyperbole and a factual statement listed in the answer options.

Understatement is the opposite of hyperbole. The device minimizes or downplays something for effect. Consider a person who climbs Mount Everest and then describes the journey as *a little stroll*. As with other types of figurative language, understatement has a range of uses. The device may convey self-deprecation or modesty as in the above example. Of course, some people might interpret understatement as false modesty (i.e., a deliberate attempt to call attention to oneself or a situation). For example, a woman is complimented on her enormous diamond engagement ring and says, *Oh, this little thing?* Her understatement might be viewed as snobby or insensitive.

> ➢ **Review Video: Hyperbole and Understatement**
> *Visit **mometrix.com/academy** and enter **Code: 308470***

A **simile** is a figurative expression that is similar to a metaphor, yet the expression requires the use of the distancing words *like* or *as*. Some examples: *The sun was like an orange*, *eager as a beaver*, and *nimble as a mountain goat*. Because a simile includes *like* or a*s,* the device creates a space between the description and the thing being described. If an author says that *a house was like a shoebox*, then the tone is different than the author saying that the house *was* a shoebox. In a simile, authors indicate an awareness that the description is not the same thing as the thing being described. In a metaphor, there is no such distinction. Authors will use metaphors and similes depending on their intended tone.

> ➢ **Review Video: Simile**
> *Visit mometrix.com/academy and enter* **Code: 642949**

Another type of figurative language is **personification.** This is the description of a nonhuman thing as if the item were human. Literally, the word means the process of making something into a person. The general intent of personification is to describe things in a manner that will be comprehensible to readers. When an author states that a tree *groans* in the wind, he or she does not mean that the tree is emitting a low, pained sound from a mouth. Instead, the author means that the tree is making a noise similar to a human groan. Of course, this personification establishes a tone of sadness or suffering. A different tone would be established if the author said that the tree was *swaying* or *dancing*.

> ➢ **Review Video: Personification**
> *Visit mometrix.com/academy and enter* **Code: 260066**

Irony is a statement that suggests the opposite of what one expects to occur. In other words, the device is used when an author or character says one thing but means another. For example, imagine a man who is covered in mud and dressed in tattered clothes and walks in his front door to meet his wife. Then, his wife asks him, "How was your day?", and he says, "Great!" The man's response to his wife is an example of irony. As in this example, irony often depends on information that the reader obtains elsewhere. There is a fine distinction between irony and sarcasm. Irony is any statement in which the literal meaning is opposite from the intended meaning. Sarcasm is similar, yet the statement is insulting to the person at whom the words are directed. A sarcastic statement suggests that the other person is foolish to believe that an obviously false statement is true.

> ➢ **Review Video: Irony**
> *Visit mometrix.com/academy and enter* **Code: 374204**

As a person is exposed to more words, the extent of their vocabulary will expand. By reading on a regular basis, a person can increase the number of ways that they have seen a word in context. Based on experience, a person can recall how a word was used in the past and apply that knowledge to a new context. For example, a person may have seen the word *gull* used to mean a bird that is found near the seashore. However, a *gull* can be a person who is tricked easily. If the word in context is used in reference to a character, the reader can recognize the insult since gulls are not seen as extremely intelligent. When you use your knowledge about a word, you can find comparisons or figure out the meaning for a new use of a word.

Verbal

The Verbal test of the SSAT consists of a total of 60 questions (30 Synonyms and 30 Analogies).

Synonyms

As part of your exam, you need to understand how words connect to each other. When you understand how words relate to each other, you will discover more in a passage. This is explained by understanding synonyms. As an example, *dry* and *arid* are synonyms, and *dry* and *wet* are antonyms. There are many pairs of words in English that can be considered synonyms, despite having slightly different definitions.

For instance, the words *friendly* and *collegial* can both be used to describe a warm interpersonal relationship, and one would be correct to call them synonyms. However, *collegial* (kin to *colleague*) is often used in reference to professional or academic relationships, and *friendly* has no such connotation.

If the difference between the two words is too great, then they should not be called synonyms. *Hot* and *warm* are not synonyms because their meanings are too distinct. A good way to determine whether two words are synonyms is to substitute one word for the other word and verify that the meaning of the sentence has not changed. Substituting *warm* for *hot* in a sentence would convey a different meaning. Although warm and hot may seem close in meaning, warm generally means that the temperature is moderate, and hot generally means that the temperature is excessively high.

> ➤ **Review Video: <u>Synonyms and Antonyms</u>**
> *Visit **mometrix.com/academy** and enter **Code: 105612**

Synonym Examples

For the Synonyms section, you will have one word and four choices for a synonym of that word. Before you look at the choices, try to think of a few words that could be a synonym for your question. Then, check the choices for a synonym of the question. Some words may seem close to the question, but you are looking for the best choice of a synonym. So, don't let your first reaction be your final decision.

<u>Example 1</u>
Insatiable:

A. Compensated
B. Content
C. Fulfilled
D. Quenched
E. Unsatisfied

Example 2
Adherent:

A. Antagonist
B. Disciple
C. Piquant
D. Submissive
E. Zealot

Example 3
Protrude:

A. Contract
B. Evocative
C. Secede
D. Swell
E. Tumult

Example 4
Unkempt:

A. Disorder
B. Flaunt
C. Volatile
D. Unblemished
E. Writhe

Answers
Example 1: E, Unsatisfied
Example 2: B, Disciple
Example 3: D, Swell
Example 4: A, Disorder

Analogies

Determine the Relationship

As you try to decide on how the words in question are connected, don't jump to understand the meaning of the words. Instead, see if you can find the relationship between the two words. To understand the relationship, you can start by creating a sentence that links the two words and puts them into perspective. At first, try to use a simple sentence to find a connection.

Then, go through each answer choice and replace the words in the answer choices with the parts of your simple sentence. Depending on the question, you may need to make changes to your sentence to make it more specific.

Example:
Wood is to fire as

Simple Sentence: *Wood* feeds a *fire* as

Wood is to fire as
    A. Farmer is to cow
    B. Gasoline is to engine

Using the simple sentence, you would state "Farmer feeds a cow" which is correct. Yet, the next answer choice "Gasoline feeds an engine" is also true. So which is the correct answer? With this simple sentence, we need to be more specific.

Specific Sentences: "Wood feeds a fire and is consumed" / "Wood is burned in a fire"

These specific sentences show that answer choice (A) is incorrect and answer choice (B) is clearly correct. With the specific sentences, you have "Gasoline feeds an engine and is consumed" is correct. Also, "Farmer feeds a cow and is consumed" is clearly incorrect.

If your simple sentence seems correct with more than one answer choice, then keep making changes until only one answer choice makes sense.

> ➤ **Review Video: <u>Determine the Relationship</u>**
> *Visit mometrix.com/academy and enter Code:* **919115**

Eliminating Similarities

This method works well in the Analogies section and the Synonyms section. You can start by looking over the answer choices and see what clues they provide. If there are any common relationships between the pairs of terms, then those answer choices have to be wrong.

Example:
Tough is to rugged as
    A.   Soft is to hard
    B.   Clear is to foggy
    C.   Inhale is to exhale
    D.   Throw is to catch
    E.   Rigid is to taut

In this example, tough and rugged are synonyms. Also, the first four answer choices are antonyms. You may not realize that taut and rigid are synonyms. However, it has to be correct. The reason is that you know the other four answer choices all had the same relationship of being antonyms.

Word Types

Example:
Gardener is to hedge as
    A.   Wind is to rock
    B.   Woodcarver is to stick

In this example, you could start with a simple sentence of "Gardener cuts away at hedges." Now, both answer choices seem correct with this sentence. For choice (A), you can say that "Wind cuts away at rocks" due to erosion. For choice (B), you can say that a "Woodcarver cuts away at sticks." The difference is that a gardener is a person, and a woodcarver is a person. However, the wind is a thing which makes answer choice (B) correct.

Face Value

When you are not sure about an answer, you should try to accept the problem at face value. Don't read too much into it. These problems will not ask you to make impossible comparisons. Truly, the SSAT test writers are not trying to throw you off with cheap tricks. If you have to make a stretch of the question to make a connection between the two terms, then you should start over and find another relationship. Don't make the problem more difficult. These are normal questions with differences in difficulty. Sometimes the terms that go together and their relationships may not be very clear. So, you will want to read over the question and answer choices carefully.
Example:
Odor is to smell as flavor is to
    A.   believe
    B.   know
    C.   feel
    D.   taste
    E.   punish

Would a flavor be "punished," "known", "felt", "tasted", or "believed"? The analogy is about a synonym. So, answer choice D which is "taste" is a synonym of flavor and is the best answer.

Read Carefully

To understand the analogies, you need to read the terms and answer choices carefully. You can miss the question because you misread the terms. Each question here has only a few words, so you can spend time reading them carefully. Yet, you cannot forget your time limit of the section. So, don't spend too much time on one question. Just focus on reading carefully and be sure to read all of the choices. You may find an answer choice that seems correct. Yet, when you finish reading over the choices, you may find a better choice.

Essay

Practice Makes Prepared Writers

Writing is a skill that continues to need development throughout a person's life. For some people, writing seems to be a natural gift. They rarely struggle with writer's block. When you read their papers, they have persuasive ideas. For others, writing is an intimidating task that they endure. As you practice, you can improve your skills and be better prepared for writing a time-sensitive essay.

Remember that you are practicing for more than an exam. Two of the most valuable things in life are the abilities to read critically and to write clearly. When you work on evaluating the arguments of a passage and explain your thoughts well, you are developing skills that you will use for a lifetime. In this overview of essay writing, you will find strategies and tools that will prepare you to write better essays.

Creative Writing

Take time to read a story or hear stories read aloud and use those opportunities to learn more about how stories are put together. This offers a frame for you to talk about a story with others and will help you to write better stories. With each new story that you read, try to predict what could happen in the story. Try to understand the setting by picturing the scenes and sounds that are described and the behaviors of characters. Then, try to summarize the events to understand more of the story.

If you need more help with understanding a story, you can try to relate narrative characters and events to your own life. For example, when reading a story, you can ask the following: Who is the main character in the story? What happened first? What happened next? What happened at the end of the story? Where does this story take place? And what is the theme or point of this story?

Establish a Context
When writing a narrative, a context for the story has to be introduced. The context could consist of a description of a situation or a setting. A point of view also has to be established. It could be introduced by a narrator and may or may not be the same as the author's. The points of view can be shown through dialogue or how the narrator reacts to or describes what characters do in the story. The characters will need to be drawn very clearly through their descriptions (i.e., what they do and what they say). You may hide his point of view in the characters' thoughts or actions. The narrator's point of view is usually more overtly seen in what is said in the narrative by the narrator.

Decide the character and point of view in the following passage.

Alma Way stared straight ahead. Her long delicate face was pale. Her gloved hands, clutching the hymn book, trembled as she sang. The time for her solo was near. She felt panic rising within her but she took a deep breath. Then her voice rang out, clear as a bell. The congregation nodded admiringly.

The author has chosen to tell the narrative from the third-person omniscient viewpoint which means the narrator is all-knowing. Readers are introduced to the character of Alma Way by the author's description of Alma. Readers can learn a lot about her from the description of how she is staring: that her face is pale and that her gloved hands clutched a hymn book. The narrator also shares that she feels panic.

Point of View
Point of view is the perspective from which writing occurs. There are several possibilities:
- *First person* is written so that the *I* of the story is a participant or observer. First-person narratives let narrators express inner feelings and thoughts. The narrator may be a close friend of the protagonist, or the narrator can be less involved with the main characters and plot.
- *Second person* is a device to draw the reader in more closely. It is really a variation or refinement of the first-person narrative. In some cases, a narrative combines both second-person and first-person voices, speaking of "you" and "I." When the narrator is also a character in the story, the narrative is better defined as first-person even though it also has addresses of "you."
- *Third person* may be either objective or subjective, and either omniscient or limited. Objective third-person narration does not include what the characters are thinking or feeling, while subjective third-person narration does include this information. The third-person omniscient narrator knows everything about all characters, including their thoughts and emotions; and all related places, times, and events. The third-person limited narrator may know everything about a particular character of focus, but is limited to that character. In other words, the narrator cannot speak about anything that character does not know.

Sequence of Events
The sequence of events in a narrative should follow naturally out of the action and the plot. Rather than being forced, the sequence should follow the natural flow of a dialogue or plot and enhance what happens in the story. The only time that the sequence is not in the order that events naturally happen is when an author decides to use the literary device called flashback. In this case the action does not flow in sequence; instead, the action jumps back and forth in time. Events in a narrative are extremely important in helping the reader understand the intent or message of a narrative, which is why it is important to take note of the way in which the plot unfolds.

Remember from the Reading section that a plot shows the order of a story. The introduction is the beginning of the story. Next, the rising action, conflict, climax, and falling action are the middle. Then, the resolution or conclusion is the ending. So, stay focused on the goal of writing a story that needs those main parts: a beginning, a middle, and an ending.

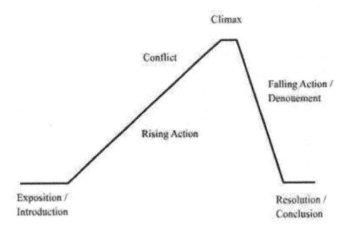

Author Techniques

You can employ many techniques to make your narrative essay come alive in a fresh and interesting way. Dialogue is an important one. Often, dialogue is the means that helps readers understand what is happening and what a character is like. Equally important are the descriptions that you can use to help readers visualize a setting and what a character looks or acts like. Remember that you have limited time to write a whole story. So, don't be concerned with providing description for everything that you put in your story.

Transitions Words

Transition words can be helpful when writing a narrative so that readers can follow the events in a seamless manner. Sequence words such as *first*, *second*, and *last* assist readers in understanding the order in which events occur. Words such as *then* or *next* also show the order in which events occur. *After a while* and *before this* are other sequence expressions.

Additionally, transition words can indicate a change from one time frame or setting to another: "We were sitting on a rock near the lake when we heard a strange sound." At this point we decided to look to see where the noise was coming from by going further into the woods." In this excerpt the phrase *at this point* signals a shift in setting between what was happening and what came next.

Precise Language

Your use of precise language, phrases, and sensory language (i.e., language that appeals to the five senses), helps readers imagine a place, situation, or person in the way that you intended. Details of character's actions, the setting, and the events in a narrative help create a lively and thought-provoking story. Sensory language helps convey the mood and feeling of the setting and characters and can highlight the theme of your story.

Read the excerpt and analyze its language.

> All through his boyhood, George Willard had been in the habit of walking on Trunion Pike. He had been there on winter nights when it was covered with snow and only the moon looked down at him; he had been there in the fall when bleak winds blew and on summer evenings when the air vibrated with the song of insects.

This excerpt is filled with precise and sensory language. The descriptions of walking on Turnion Pike *when it was covered with snow and only the moon looked down*, of the *bleak winds* that blew, and times that *the air vibrated with the song of insects* all contribute to bring the words to life and allows readers to see what the author envisioned by creating images through vivid and precise language. The description of the setting uses relevant details that readers can use to understand something about George Willard.

Role of a Conclusion

The conclusion of a narrative is extremely important because it shapes the entire story and is the resolution of the characters' conflict(s). Some conclusions may be tragic (e.g., classic tragedies), and other endings may be lighthearted (e.g., classic comedies). Modern stories tend to have endings that are more complex than the clear-cut endings of classic literature. They often leave readers without a clear sense of how a character fares at the end. Nonetheless, this element can show how life is not always clear in its conclusions.

A student is writing a story about a girl who wants to be on the basketball team and works out every day to get in shape. The student has written about the girl's feelings and the obstacles she has had to overcome. Now, a conclusion is needed for the story. Describe what needs to be done to develop a good conclusion.

> The student should think about the character as though the girl were a real person because this seems to be a realistic story. The student should think about what he or she wants to have as the story's theme. Does the student want to show that hard work pays off? Or is the goal to show that you cannot always get what you want even with hard work? In other words, the student has to decide whether the story will have a happy ending or not. Whatever kind of an ending the student decides upon, the conclusion should bring the entire story to a fitting and appropriate end so that readers have a sense of closure.

Traditional Essay Overview

A traditional way to prepare for the writing section is to read. When you read newspapers, magazines, and books, you learn about new ideas. You can read newspapers and magazines to become informed about issues that affect many people.

As you think about those issues and ideas, you can take a position and form opinions. Try to develop these ideas and your opinions by sharing them with friends. After you develop your opinions, try writing them down as if you were going to spread your ideas beyond your friends.

For your exam you need to write an essay that shows your ability to understand and respond to an assignment. When you talk with others, you give beliefs, opinions, and ideas about the world around you. As you talk, you have the opportunity to share information with spoken words, facial expressions, or hand motions. If your audience seems confused about your ideas, you can stop and explain. However, when you write, you have a different assignment. As you write, you need to share information in a clear, precise way. Your readers will not have the chance to ask questions about your ideas. So, before you write your essay, you need to understand the assignment. As you write, you should be clear and precise about your ideas.

Brainstorm

Spend the first three to five minutes brainstorming for ideas. Write down any ideas that you might have on the topic. The purpose is to pull any helpful information from the depths of your memory. In this stage, anything goes down on note paper regardless of how good or bad the idea may seem at first glance. You may not bring your own paper for these notes. Instead, you will be provided with paper at the time of your test.

Strength through Different Viewpoints

The best papers will contain several examples and mature reasoning. As you brainstorm, you should consider different perspectives. There are more than two sides to every topic. In an argument, there are countless perspectives that can be considered. On any topic, different groups are impacted and many reach the same conclusion or position. Yet, they reach the same conclusion through different paths. Before writing your essay, try to *see* the topic through as many different *eyes* as you can.

Once you have finished with your creative flow, you need to stop and review what you brainstormed. *Which idea allowed you to come up with the most supporting information?* Be sure to pick an angle that will allow you to have a thorough coverage of the prompt.

Every garden of ideas has weeds. The ideas that you brainstormed are going to be random pieces of information of different values. Go through the pieces carefully and pick out the ones that are the best. The best ideas are strong points that will be easy to write a paragraph in response.

Now, you have your main ideas that you will focus on. So, align them in a sequence that will flow in a smooth, sensible path from point to point. With this approach, readers will go smoothly from one idea to the next in a reasonable order. Readers want an essay that has a sense of continuity (i.e., Point 1 to Point 2 to Point 3 and so on).

Start Your Engines

Now, you have a logical flow of the main ideas for the start of your essay. Begin by expanding on the first point, then move to your second point. Pace yourself. Don't spend too much time on any one of the ideas that you are expanding on. You want to have time for all of them. *Make sure that you watch your time.* If you have twenty minutes left to write out your ideas and you have four ideas, then you can only use five minutes per idea. Writing so much information in so little time can be an intimidating task. Yet, when you pace yourself, you can get through all of your points. If you find that you are falling behind, then you can remove one of your weaker arguments. This will allow you to give enough support to your remaining paragraphs.

Once you finish expanding on an idea, go back to your brainstorming session where you wrote out your ideas. You can scratch through the ideas as you write about them. This will let you see what you need to write about next and what you have left to cover.

Your introductory paragraph should have several easily identifiable features.

- First, the paragraph should have a quick description or paraphrasing of the topic. Use your own words to briefly explain what the topic is about.
- Second, you should list your writing points. What are the main ideas that you came up with earlier? If someone was to read only your introduction, they should be able to get a good summary of the entire paper.
- Third, you should explain your opinion of the topic and give an explanation for why you feel that way. What is your decision or conclusion on the topic?

Each of your following paragraphs should develop one of the points listed in the main paragraph. Use your personal experience and knowledge to support each of your points. Examples should back up everything.

Once you have finished expanding on each of your main points, you need to conclude your essay. Summarize what you written in a conclusion paragraph. Explain once more your argument on the prompt and review why you feel that way in a few sentences. At this stage, you have already backed up your statements. So, there is no need to do that again. You just need to refresh your readers on the main points that you made in your essay.

Don't Panic

Whatever you do during the essay, do not panic. When you panic, you will put fewer words on the page and your ideas will be weak. Therefore, panicking is not helpful. If your mind goes blank when you see the prompt, then you need to take a deep breath. Remember to brainstorm and put anything on scratch paper that comes to mind.

Also, don't get clock fever. You may be overwhelmed when you're looking at a page that is mostly blank. Your mind is full of random thoughts and feeling confused, and the clock is ticking down faster. You have already brainstormed for ideas. Therefore, you don't have to keep coming up with ideas. If you're running out of time and you have a lot of ideas that you haven't written down, then don't be afraid to make some cuts. Start picking the best ideas that you have left and expand on them. Don't feel like you have to write on all of your ideas.

A short paper that is well written and well organized is better than a long paper that is poorly written and poorly organized. Don't keep writing about a subject just to add sentences and avoid repeating a statement or idea that you have explained already. The goal is 1 to 2 pages of quality writing. That is your target, but you should not mess up your paper by trying to get there. You want to have a natural end to your work without having to cut something short. If your essay is a little long, then that isn't a problem as long as your ideas are clear and flow well from paragraph to paragraph. Remember to expand on the ideas that you identified in the brainstorming session.

Leave time at the end (at least three minutes) to go back and check over your work. Reread and make sure that everything you've written makes sense and flows well. Clean up any spelling or grammar mistakes. Also, go ahead and erase any brainstorming ideas that you weren't able to include. Then, clean up any extra information that you might have written that doesn't fit into your paper.

As you proofread, make sure that there aren't any fragments or run-ons. Check for sentences that are too short or too long. If the sentence is too short, then look to see if you have a specific subject and an active verb. If it is too long, then break up the long sentence into two sentences. Watch out for any "big words" that you may have used. Be sure that you are using difficult words correctly. Don't misunderstand; you should try to increase your vocabulary and use difficult words in your essay. However, your focus should be on developing and expressing ideas in a clear and precise way.

The Short Overview
Depending on your preferences and personality, the essay may be your hardest or your easiest section. You are required to go through the entire process of writing a paper in a limited amount of time which is very challenging.

Stay focused on each of the steps for brainstorming. Go through the process of creative flow first. You can start by generating ideas about the prompt. Next, organize those ideas into a smooth flow. Then, pick out the ideas that are the best from your list.

Create a recognizable essay structure in your paper. Start with an introduction that explains what you have decided to argue. Then, choose your main points. Use the body paragraphs to touch on those main points and have a conclusion that wraps up the topic.

Save a few moments to go back and review what you have written. Clean up any minor mistakes that you might have made and make those last few critical touches that can make a huge difference. Finally, be proud and confident of what you have written!

Practice Test

Writing

Review the following prompts and choose to write a creative story or a traditional essay. You have 25 minutes to write a creative story or respond to the traditional essay prompt.

<u>Creative Writing</u>

> "Never throughout history has a man who lived a life of ease left a name worth remembering."
> -Theodore Roosevelt

Think carefully about this quote and some of the great things that have been accomplished by living a life of difficulty. Then, write a creative story that covers the importance of working hard to accomplish great things.

<u>Traditional Essay</u>
Prompt: Some people feel that video games actually promote intelligence. They say that strategy games force players to make strategic choices, plan ahead, and react in appropriate ways to challenges. Others feel that video games are simply a mindless pastime, and that time would be better spent doing something constructive like reading or participating in sports.

Write an essay to a parent who is deciding whether they should allow their child to play video games. Take a position on whether video games are a valuable activity or simply a waste of time. Use arguments and examples to support your position.

Section 1: Quantitative

1. Jerry needs to load four pieces of equipment onto a factory elevator that has a weight limit of 800 pounds. Jerry weighs 200 pounds. What would the average weight of each item have to be so that the elevator's weight limit is not exceeded?
   a. 128 pounds
   b. 150 pounds
   c. 175 pounds
   d. 180 pounds
   e. 185 pounds

2. Chan receives a bonus from his job. He pays 30% in taxes, gives 20% to charity, uses another 20% to pay off an old debt, and sets aside 10% in a savings account. He has $600 remaining from his bonus. What was the total amount of Chan's bonus?
   a. $2400
   b. $2800
   c. $3000
   d. $3600
   e. $3800

3. A jar contains pennies and nickels. The ratio of nickels to pennies is 6:2. What percent of the coins are pennies?
   a. 25%
   b. 33.3%
   c. 40%
   d. 50%
   e. 75%

4. Given the equation, $ax + b = c$, what is the value of x?
   a. $\dfrac{c+b}{a}$

   b. $\dfrac{ca}{b}$

   c. $c - ba$

   d. $\dfrac{c-b}{a}$

   e. $\dfrac{cb}{a}$

5. If c is to be chosen at random from the set $\{1, 2, 3, 4\}$ and d is to be chosen at random from the set $\{1, 2, 3, 4\}$, what is the probability cd will be odd?
   a. $\dfrac{1}{4}$

   b. $\dfrac{1}{3}$

   c. $\dfrac{3}{4}$

   d. 2

   e. 4

6. If $x = 2y - 3$ and $2x + \frac{1}{2}y = 3$, then $y = ?$

   a. $-\frac{2}{3}$

   b. 1

   c. 2

   d. $\frac{18}{7}$

   e. 3

7. A bag contains 14 blue, 6 red, 12 green and 8 purple buttons. 25 buttons are removed from the bag randomly. How many of the removed buttons were red if the chance of drawing a red button from the bag is now $\frac{1}{3}$?

   a. 0
   b. 1
   c. 3
   d. 5
   e. 6

8. The sides of a triangle are equal to integral numbers of units. Two sides are 4 and 6 units long, respectively; what is the minimum value for the triangle's perimeter?

   a. 9 units
   b. 10 units
   c. 11 units
   d. 12 units
   e. 13 units

9. The average of six numbers is 4. If the average of two of those numbers is 2, what is the average of the other four numbers?

   a. 3
   b. 4
   c. 5
   d. 7
   e. 8

10. There are 64 squares on a checkerboard. Bobby puts one penny on the first square, two on the second square, four on the third, eight on the fourth. He continues to double the number of coins at each square until he has covered all 64 squares. How many coins must he place on the last square?

   a. 2^{63}
   b. $2^{63} + 1$
   c. $2^{63} - 1$
   d. $2^{64} - 1$
   e. 2^{64}

11. The length of Square A is 3 feet longer than the length of Square B. If the difference between their areas is 75 ft², what is the length of Square B?
  a. 6 feet
  b. 9 feet
  c. 10 feet
  d. 11 feet
  e. 12 feet

12. The cost, in dollars, of shipping x computers to California for sale is 3000 + 100x. The amount received when selling these computers is 400x dollars. What is the least number of computers that must be shipped and sold so that the amount received is at least equal to the shipping cost?
  a. 10
  b. 15
  c. 20
  d. 25
  e. 30

13. If $\frac{x}{8} = \frac{y}{4} = 4$, what is the value of $x - y$?
  a. 8
  b. 16
  c. 24
  d. 32
  e. 48

14. The scientific notation for a red blood cell is approximately 7.4 x 10⁻⁴ centimeters in diameter. What is that amount in standard form?
  a. 0.00074
  b. 0.0074
  c. 7.40000
  d. 296
  e. 7400

15. What is the area of the shaded region? (Each square represents one unit.)

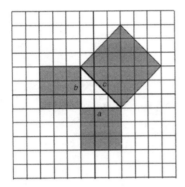

    a. 12
    b. 13
    c. 15
    d. 16
    e. 18

16. 5 more than 6 times a number is 77. What is the number?
    a. 12
    b. 17
    c. 19
    d. 24
    e. 72

17. Simplify $(3 \times 10^4) \times (2 \times 10^5)$.
    a. 5×10^9
    b. 5×10^{20}
    c. 6×10^9
    d. 6×10^{12}
    e. 6×10^{20}

18. Which of the following represents the factors of the expression, $x^2 + 3x - 28$?
    a. $(x - 14)(x + 2)$
    b. $(x + 6)(x - 3)$
    c. $(x + 4)(x - 1)$
    d. $(x - 4)(x + 7)$
    e. $(x - 14)(x + 7)$

19. Given $x^2 - 7x + 10 \geq 0$, what is the solution set for x?
    a. $2 \leq x \leq 5$
    b. $x \leq 2$ or $x \geq 5$
    c. $7 \leq x \leq 10$
    d. $x \leq 7$ or $x \geq 10$
    e. $7 \leq x \leq 5$

20. Equation A is $5y - 100x = 25$. What are the slope and y-intercept of the line?
    a. The slope is 100, and the y-intercept is 5.
    b. The slope is 5, and the y-intercept is 100.
    c. The slope is 20, and the y-intercept is 5.
    d. The slope is 25, and the y-intercept is 5.
    e. The slope is 5, and the y-intercept is 20.

21. The Charleston Recycling Company collects 50,000 tons of recyclable material every month. The chart shows the kinds of materials that are collected by the company's five trucks.

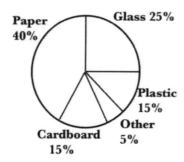

About how much paper is recycled every month?
    a. 15,000 tons
    b. 20,000 tons
    c. 25,000 tons
    d. 40,000 tons
    e. 50,000 tons

22. The volume of a rectangular box is found by multiplying its length, width, and height. If the dimensions of a box are $\sqrt{3}$, $2\sqrt{5}$, and 4, what is its volume?
    a. $2\sqrt{60}$
    b. $4\sqrt{15}$
    c. $8\sqrt{15}$
    d. $24\sqrt{5}$
    e. $8\sqrt{5}$

23. Simplify $(8 \times 10^3) + (1 \times 10^3)$.
    a. 8×10^3
    b. 8×10^6
    c. 9×10^3
    d. 9×10^6
    e. 9×10^9

24. Which function represents the graph?

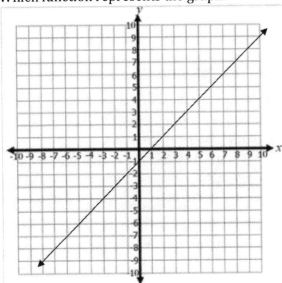

a. $y = x + 1$
b. $y = x - 1$
c. $y = -x + 1$
d. $y = -x - 1$
e. $y = 1$

25. A dress is marked down by 20% and placed on a clearance rack, on which is posted a sign reading, "Take an extra 25% off already reduced merchandise." What fraction of the original price is the final sales price of the dress?

a. $\dfrac{2}{5}$

b. $\dfrac{9}{20}$

c. $\dfrac{10}{20}$

d. $\dfrac{11}{20}$

e. $\dfrac{3}{5}$

Section 2: Reading Comprehension

Pride and Prejudice by Jane Austen:

It is a truth universally acknowledged, that a single man in possession of a good fortune, must be in want of a wife.

However little known the feelings or views of such a man may be on his first entering a neighbourhood, this truth is so well fixed in the minds of the surrounding families, that he is considered the rightful property of some one or other of their daughters.

"My dear Mr. Bennet," said his lady to him one day, "have you heard that Netherfield Park is let at last?"

Mr. Bennet replied that he had not.

"But it is," returned she; "for Mrs. Long has just been here, and she told me all about it."

Mr. Bennet made no answer.

"Do you not want to know who has taken it?" cried his wife impatiently.

"You want to tell me, and I have no objection to hearing it."

This was invitation enough.

"Why, my dear, you must know, Mrs. Long says that Netherfield is taken by a young man of large fortune from the north of England; that he came down on Monday in a chaise and four to see the place, and was so much delighted with it, that he agreed with Mr. Morris immediately; that he is to take possession before Michaelmas, and some of his servants are to be in the house by the end of next week."

"What is his name?"

"Bingley."

"Is he married or single?"

"Oh! Single, my dear, to be sure! A single man of large fortune; four or five thousand a year. What a fine thing for our girls!"

"How so? How can it affect them?"

"My dear Mr. Bennet," replied his wife, "how can you be so tiresome!" You must know that I am thinking of his marrying one of them."

"Is that his design in settling here?"

"Design! Nonsense, how can you talk so! But it is very likely that he may fall in love with one of them, and therefore you must visit him as soon as he comes."

"I see no occasion for that. You and the girls may go, or you may send them by themselves, which perhaps will be still better, for as you are as handsome as any of them, Mr. Bingley may like you the best of the party."

1. What is the central idea of this selection?
   a. A new neighbor is due to arrive who may become good friends with Mr. and Mrs. Bennet.
   b. A new neighbor is due to arrive who may be a prospective husband for one of the Bennet daughters.
   c. A new neighbor is due to arrive who may be a good business connection for Mr. Bennet.
   d. A new neighbor is due to arrive who has expressed an interest in marrying one of the Bennet daughters.
   e. A new neighbor is due to arrive who has expressed an interest in purchasing more property

2. How does Mrs. Bennet feel about the arrival of Mr. Bingley?
    a. Mrs. Bennet is excited about the arrival of Mr. Bingley.
    b. Mrs. Bennet is nervous about the arrival of Mr. Bingley.
    c. Mrs. Bennet is afraid the arrival of Mr. Bingley will upset Mr. Bennet.
    d. Mrs. Bennet is indifferent to the arrival of Mr. Bingley.
    e. Mrs. Bennet is skeptical about the arrival of Mr. Bingley.

3. Which of the following statements best describes Mrs. Bennet's feelings about her husband as indicated by this selection?
    a. Mrs. Bennet is tired of her husband.
    b. Mrs. Bennet is exasperated by her husband.
    c. Mrs. Bennet is afraid of her husband.
    d. Mrs. Bennet is indifferent toward her husband.
    e. Mrs. Bennet is bored with her husband.

4. "It is a truth universally acknowledged, that a single man in possession of a good fortune, must be in want of a wife."
Which of the following most nearly matches the meaning of the underlined phrase?
    a. Everyone knows
    b. The universe has decided
    c. It is a documented fact
    d. It is best to tell the truth
    e. Some may not recall

5. "Is that his design in settling here?"
What does the word design mean in the context of this selection?
    a. Policy
    b. Drawing
    c. Creation
    d. Improvisation
    e. Intention

Helen Keller

Helen Keller was born on June 27, 1880. She was a happy and healthy child until the age of 19 months when she fell ill with a terrible fever. Although Helen recovered from the fever, it left her both deaf and blind.

Helen was loved and cared for by her doting parents, but her behavior became erratic after she lost her hearing and sight, with unpredictable outbursts of temper. Her parents were at a loss how to reach her and teach her how to behave. Helen herself was frustrated and lonely in her dark, silent world. All of that began to change in March 1887 when Anne Sullivan came to live with the Kellers and be Helen's teacher.

Anne taught Helen to communicate by forming letters with her fingers held in another person's hand. In this way, Teacher, as Helen called her, taught her pupil to spell cake, doll, and milk. However, it was not until Anne spelled w-a-t-e-r in Helen's hands as cold water gushed over both of them that Helen made the exciting connection between the words and the world around her. This connection engendered an insatiable curiosity within Helen. After that day, Helen learned at an incredible rate with Teacher by her side.

Helen went on to graduate from Radcliffe College. She became a famous writer, speaker, and advocate. The story of Helen's remarkable life is known worldwide. Anne Sullivan and Helen Keller were inseparable until Anne's death in 1936. Teacher shined a light in Helen's dark world and showed her the way.

6. Which organizational pattern does the author use?
   a. Comparison and contrast
   b. Chronological order
   c. Cause and effect
   d. Problem/solution
   e. No apparent pattern

7. What is the author's primary purpose in writing this passage?
   a. To inform people about Helen Keller's college career
   b. To inform people about Anne Sullivan's life
   c. To inform people about services available for the deaf and blind
   d. To inform people about overcoming incredible obstacles
   e. To inform people about Helen Keller's life

8. How does the author make a connection between the second and third paragraphs?
   a. The author begins the third paragraph by continuing to talk about Helen's parents who were introduced in the second paragraph.
   b. The author organizes the second and third paragraphs the same way.
   c. The author ends the second paragraph with the advent of Anne Sullivan in Helen's life, and begins the third paragraph with the most important contribution Anne made to Helen's education.
   d. The author uses the third paragraph to elaborate on Helen's frustration and resulting temper tantrums introduced in the second paragraph.
   e. The author continues to use the theme of teamwork throughout both paragraphs

9. What is the author's tone in this passage?
   a. Indifferent
   b. Censorious
   c. Admiring
   d. Impartial
   e. Informational

10. What was the turning point in Helen's life?
   a. When Helen learned to connect feeling water on her hands with the word "water."
   b. When Helen graduated from Radcliffe College.
   c. When Helen contracted the fever that took away her hearing and sight.
   d. When Anne Sullivan came to live with the Kellers and be Helen's teacher.
   e. When Anne Sullivan taught Helen to spell cake, doll, and milk.

11. Which of the following can you infer was true about Helen's parents?
    a. Helen's parents were frustrated that they were unable to help Helen communicate.
    b. Helen's parents were jealous that Anne Sullivan was closer to Helen than they were.
    c. Helen's parents were glad to give Anne Sullivan full responsibility for Helen.
    d. Helen's parents wanted their daughter to graduate from Radcliffe College.
    e. Helen's parents wished that they had contacted Anne Sullivan sooner.

Annelids

The phylum Annelida, named for the Latin word *anellus*, meaning "ring", includes earthworms, leeches, and other similar organisms. In their typical form, these animals exhibit bilateral symmetry, a cylindrical cross section, and an elongate body divided externally into segments (*metameres*) by a series of rings (*annuli*). They are segmented internally as well, with most of the internal organs repeated in series in each segment. This organization is termed *metamerism*. Metameric segmentation is the distinguishing feature of this phylum, and provides it with a degree of evolutionary plasticity in that certain segments can be modified and specialized to perform specific functions. For example, in some species certain of the locomotor *parapodia*, or feet, may be modified for grasping, and some portions of the gut may evolve digestive specializations.

The gut is a straight, muscular tube that functions independently of the muscular activity in the body wall. The Annelida resemble the nematodes, another worm phylum, in possessing a fluid-filled internal cavity separating the gut from the body wall. In both phyla, this cavity is involved in locomotion. However, in the annelids this space is formed at a much later time during the development of the embryo, and presumably evolved much later as well. This fluid-filled internal space is called a true *coelom*.

The annelid excretory and circulatory systems are well developed, and some members of the phylum have evolved respiratory organs. The nervous system offers a particular example of metameric specialization. It is concentrated anteriorly into enlarged cerebral ganglia connected to a ventral nerve cord that extends posteriorly and is organized into repeating segmental ganglia.

This phylum includes members bearing adaptations required for aquatic (marine or freshwater) or terrestrial habitats. They may be free-living entities or exist as parasites. Among the best known are the earthworm *Lumbricus*, the water leech *Hirudo*, and the marine worm *Nereis*.

12 What is the purpose of this passage?
    a. To describe the annelid nervous system.
    b. To describe the annelid digestive system.
    c. To introduce distinctive features of annelid anatomy.
    d. To define metamerism.
    e. To review the evolution of annelids

13. One evolutionary advantage of segmentation is that
    a. Segmented animals have many feet.
    b. Segmented animals have a fluid-filled coelom.
    c. These animals are able to move at a faster rate than previous annelids.
    d. These animals are now able to have aquatic or terrestrial habitats.
    e. Parts of some segments can become specialized to perform certain functions.

14. The main difference between the Annelida and all other animal phyla is that
    a. the Annelida are worms.
    b. the Annelida include the leeches.
    c. the Annelida are metameric.
    d. the Annelida are aquatic.
    e. the Annelida's excretory and circulatory systems.

15. The purpose of the last paragraph in the passage is to
    a. give familiar examples of members of the annelid phylum.
    b. show that annelids may be parasites.
    c. tell the reader that annelids may be adapted to aquatic environments.
    d. show that there are many annelids in nature and that they are adapted to a wide variety of habitats.
    e. None of the above

16. The second paragraph discusses annelids and nematodes. Which relationship(s) between these two phyla does the author establish by describing their respective characteristics?
    a. Comparison
    b. Contrast
    c. Cause and Effect
    d. Comparison and Contrast
    e. None of the above

17. After the first sentence, which of the following describes the structure of this passage relative to the paragraph content sequence?
    a. Body parts; body systems; types, habitats, names; distinctive feature
    b. Distinctive feature; body parts; body systems; types, habitats, names
    c. Body systems; distinctive feature; types, habitats, names; body parts
    d. Types, habitats, names; distinctive feature; body parts; body systems
    e. Types, habitats, names; body parts; body systems; distinctive feature

The Thought-Fox by Ted Hughes

I imagine this midnight moment's forest:
Something else is alive
Beside the clock's loneliness
And this blank page where my fingers move.

Through the window I see no star:
Something more near
Though deeper within darkness
Is entering the loneliness:

Cold, delicately as the dark snow
A fox's nose touches twig, leaf;
Two eyes serve a movement, that now
And again now, and now, and now

Sets neat prints into the snow
Between trees, and warily a lame
Shadow lags by stump and in hollow
Of a body that is bold to come

Across clearings, an eye,
A widening deepening greenness,
Brilliantly, concentratedly,
Coming about its own business

Till, with a sudden sharp hot stink of fox,
It enters the dark hole of the head.
The window is starless still; the clock ticks,
The page is printed.

18. The primary literary device used by the poet here is...
    a. Foreshadowing
    b. Irony
    c. Clichés
    d. Metaphor
    e. Allusion

19. Which of these does this poem really describe?
    a. The process of a fox's natural actions
    b. The process of being inspired by nature
    c. The process of being inspired to write
    d. The process of being attacked by a fox
    e. The process of working in a print shop

20. Which of the following best characterizes how this poem portrays the creative process?
    a. The poet exercises tight control of a thought.
    b. The poet finds his best writing when visiting forests.
    c. The poet carefully guides the thought to him.
    d. The poet imagines a fox to help him to write.
    e. The poet is a passive recipient of the thought.

"The Gettysburg Address" by Abraham Lincoln

Four score and seven years ago our fathers brought forth, upon this continent, a new nation, conceived in Liberty, and dedicated to the proposition that all men are created equal.

Now we are engaged in a great civil war, testing whether that nation, or any nation so conceived, and so dedicated, can long endure. We are met here on a great battlefield of that war. We have come to dedicate a portion of it as a final resting place for those who here gave their lives that that nation might live. It is altogether fitting and proper that we should do this.

But in a larger sense we cannot dedicate - we cannot consecrate - we cannot hallow this ground. The brave men, living and dead, who struggled here, have consecrated it far above our poor power to add or detract. The world will little note, nor long remember, what we say here, but can never forget what they did here.

It is for us, the living, rather to be dedicated here to the unfinished work which they have, thus far, so nobly carried on. It is rather for us to be here dedicated to the great task remaining before us - that from these honored dead we take increased devotion to that cause for which they here gave the last full measure of devotion - that we here highly resolve that these dead shall not have died in vain; that this nation shall have a new birth of freedom; and that this government of the people, by the people, for the people, shall not perish from the earth.

21. What is the main message of this speech?
    a. Those who died in this battle honor this land we are dedicating today better than anyone else.
    b. As we honor those who died in this battle, we should move forward with renewed dedication to ensuring the nation our founding fathers created continues to function the way they intended.
    c. We need to put the regrets of the past aside, without remembering the sacrifices of those who gave their lives for our country.
    d. The war we are fighting is far from over, as evidenced by the number of lives lost in this battle.
    e. The struggle to make this battle a historic one will be a long fight. We must ensure that the people who paid the ultimate price are remembered

22. The phrase "the world will little note" means what?
    a. The world will not soon forget.
    b. The world will record what we say here.
    c. The world will not spread this information to distant places.
    d. The world will recall what we do with perfect accuracy.
    e. The world will not pay much attention.

23. There were nearly 100 years between the American Revolution and the Civil War. The speech connects ideas about these two conflicts by saying that the ideas of the Civil War
    a. threaten those of the Revolution.
    b. are similar to those of the Revolution.
    c. are newer than those of the Revolution.
    d. are better than those of the Revolution.
    e. are incomparable to those of the Revolution.

24. Why does Lincoln most likely talk about the past before he talks about the present?
    a. to incite listeners of his message to protest
    b. to remember what has been lost in the past
    c. to establish context for his main message
    d. to try to get listeners to side with his position
    e. to appeal to the audience's patriotism and loyalty

25. What is the following sentence addressing?

Now we are engaged in a great civil war, testing whether that nation, or any nation so conceived, and so dedicated, can long endure.

    a. whether or not a nation based on ideas of freedom and equality can survive for any significant length of time
    b. whether or not the Union will be able to preserve the existing structure of the United States by preventing the Confederacy from seceding
    c. whether or not the Confederacy will be successful in seceding from the United States and surviving on its own
    d. whether or not Lincoln should continue dedicating troops to the war
    e. None of the above

26. In line 15, the word "vain" most nearly means:
    a. decisive
    b. frivolous
    c. momentous
    d. practical
    e. important

<u>Close Relationships in the 21st Century</u>
    We all know the drill: the consequences of urban sprawl, American's long work hours, and devotion to television and the internet are doing nothing good for American communities.

    A new study by sociologists at Duke University and the University of Arizona adds more grist to this mill, noting that Americans in 2004 had smaller networks of people with whom they talk about matters important to them than they did in 1985. (*Social Isolation in America: Changes in Core Discussion Networks Over Two Decades*, American Sociological Review, June 2006.) In 1985, Americans had three confidants, in 2004, we averaged two. The number of Americans who had no one with whom to talk about important matters almost doubled in 2004 to over 25%. Increasingly, most confidants are family: in 2004,

80% of people talked only to family about important matters and about 9% people depended totally on their spouse.

This decrease in confidants is part (a result) of the same trend that's leaving fewer people knowing their neighbors or participating in social clubs or public affairs than in the past (phenomena noted in the book Better Together: Restoring the American Community by Robert Putnam and Lewis Feldstein). We know a lot of people, but not necessarily very well.

Left to our own devices and cultural trends then, we seem to be moving in an unpleasant direction. Communities are formed ad hoc, around specific shared individual interests. This wouldn't be bad, of course, except that those communities seem to exist only within the constraints of those shared interests, and don't develop into close and meaningful relationships. The transient and specific nature of many of our relationships today can keep us socially busy without building the lasting relationships and communities that we want.

So what do we do about it if we want to change things? Harvard University's School of Government put together 150 ways to increase what they call "social capital" (i.e., the value of our social networks). Among their suggestions are: support local merchants; audition for community theater or volunteer to usher; participate in political campaigns; start or join a carpool; eat breakfast at a local gathering spot on Saturdays; and stop and make sure the person on the side of the highway is OK.

27. According to the author, which of the following was true in 2004:
   a. The average American had three confidants and 9% of people depended totally on their spouse for discussion of important matters.
   b. The average American had two confidants, and 80% of people discussed important matters only with their spouses.
   c. The average American had two confidants, and 9% of people discussed important matters only with family members.
   d. The average American had two confidants, and 80% of people discussed important matters only with family members.
   e. The average American had three confidants, and 80% of people depended totally on their spouse for discussion of important matters.

28. The author argues that the transient nature of many of today's relationships is problematic because:
   a. we don't share specific interests
   b. we don't know many people
   c. it prevents us building lasting relationships and communities
   d. we have too much social capital
   e. we are overcommitted in our personal and professional lives

29. Which of the following are some of the causes to which the author attributes problems in American communities:
    a. too much homework and devotion to television
    b. urban sprawl and long work hours
    c. long work hours and growth of exercise
    d. urban sprawl and decline of sports team membership
    e. long work hours and too much homework

30. Which of the following is not something the author states was suggested by Harvard University as a way to increase social capital:
    a. eat breakfast at a local gathering spot
    b. join a bowling team
    c. support local merchants
    d. join a carpool
    e. audition for community theater

31. How many ways did Harvard University's School of Government suggest to increase social capital?
    a. 25
    b. 50
    c. 80
    d. 100
    e. 150

An Excerpt from "To Build a Fire" by Jack London

But all this—the mysterious, far-reaching hair-line trail, the absence of sun from the sky, the tremendous cold, and the strangeness and weirdness of it all—made no impression on the man. It was not because he was long used to it. He was a newcomer in the land, a chechaquo, and this was his first winter. The trouble with him was that he was without imagination. He was quick and alert in the things of life, but only in the things, and not in the significances. Fifty degrees below zero meant eighty-odd degrees of frost. Such fact impressed him as being cold and uncomfortable, and that was all. It did not lead him to meditate upon his frailty as a creature of temperature, and upon man's frailty in general, able only to live within certain narrow limits of heat and cold; and from there on it did not lead him to the conjectural field of immortality and man's place in the universe. Fifty degrees below zero stood for a bite of frost that hurt and that must be guarded against by the use of mittens, ear-flaps, warm moccasins, and thick socks. Fifty degrees below zero was to him just precisely fifty degrees below zero. That there should be anything more to it than that was a thought that never entered his head.

. . . .

At the man's heels trotted a dog, a big native husky, the proper wolf-dog, gray-coated and without any visible or temperamental difference from its brother, the wild wolf. The animal was depressed by the tremendous cold. It knew that it was no time for travelling. Its instinct told it a truer tale than was told to the man by the man's judgment. In reality, it was not merely colder than fifty below zero; it was colder than sixty below, than seventy below. It was seventy-five below zero. Since the freezing-point is thirty-two above zero, it meant that one hundred and seven degrees of frost obtained. The dog did not know anything about thermometers. Possibly in its brain there was no sharp consciousness of a condition of very cold such as was in the man's brain. But the brute had its instinct. It experienced a vague but menacing apprehension that subdued it and made it slink along at the man's heels, and that made it question eagerly every unwonted movement of the man as if expecting him to go into camp or to seek shelter somewhere and build a fire. The dog had learned fire, and it wanted fire, or else to burrow under the snow and cuddle its warmth away from the air.

32. In the story that this passage comes from, the main character struggles against the cold and eventually freezes to death. Given this information, which of the following devices is the author using in the first paragraph?
    a. First person point of view
    b. Hyperbole
    c. Onomatopoeia
    d. Foreshadowing
    e. Symbolism

33. What is the point of view used in this passage?
    a. First person
    b. First person plural
    c. Unreliable narrator
    d. Third person omniscient
    e. Third person limited

34. In what sense should the passage be taken when it mentions immortality and man's place in the universe?
    a. Humans are frail
    b. Humans are stronger than nature
    c. Humans will one day attain immortality
    d. Humans are smarter than animals
    e. Human inventions will always protect mankind from nature

35. In what way does the narrator say the dog is better off than the man?
    a. The dog is better equipped for the cold because of its fur.
    b. The dog has a better conscious idea of what the cold means
    c. The dog's instinct guides it, while the man's intellect fails him
    d. The dog understands mankind's place in the universe
    e. The dog is humble before nature

Comets

Comets are bodies that orbit the sun. They are distinguishable from asteroids by the presence of coma or tails. In the outer solar system, comets remain frozen and are so small that they are difficult to detect from Earth. As a comet approaches the inner solar system, solar radiation causes the materials within the comet to vaporize and trail off the nuclei. The released dust and gas forms a fuzzy atmosphere called the coma, and the force exerted on the coma causes a tail to form, pointing away from the sun.

Comet nuclei are made of ice, dust, rock and frozen gases and vary widely in size: from 100 meters or so to tens of kilometers across. The comas may be even larger than the Sun. Because of their low mass, they do not become spherical and have irregular shapes.

There are over 3,500 known comets, and the number is steadily increasing. This represents only a small portion of the total comets existing, however. Most comets are too faint to be visible without the aid of a telescope; the number of comets visible to the naked eye is around one a year.

Comets leave a trail of solid debris behind them. If a comet's path crosses the Earth's path, there will likely be meteor showers as Earth passes through the trail of debris.

Many comets and asteroids have collided into Earth. Some scientists believe that comets hitting Earth about 4 billion years ago brought a significant proportion of the water in Earth's oceans. There are still many near-Earth comets.

Most comets have oval shaped orbits that take them close to the Sun for part of their orbit and then out further into the Solar System for the remainder of the orbit. Comets are often classified according to the length of their orbital period: short period comets have orbital periods of less than 200 years, long period comets have orbital periods of more than 200 years, single apparition comets have trajectories which cause them to permanently leave the solar system after passing the Sun once.

36. What does the passage claim distinguishes comets from asteroids?
    a. The make-up of their nuclei
    b. The presence of coma or tails
    c. Their orbital periods
    d. Their irregular shapes
    e. Their classification system

37. According to the passage, which of the following is true?
    a. There are 350 known comets and the number is steadily increasing.
    b. There are 3,500 known comets and the number is staying the same.
    c. There are 3,500 known comets and many more comets that aren't known.
    d. Most comets are visible to the naked eye.
    e. None of the above

38. According to the passage, why do comets have irregular shapes?
    a. because they are not spherical
    b. because they have orbital periods
    c. because of their low mass
    d. because of their tails
    e. because they are made of ice and frozen gases

39. What does the passage claim about the size of comets?
    a. Some are tens of kilometers across and can be seen without the use of a telescope
    b. Some are tens of kilometers across and the coma is never larger than the Sun
    c. Some are 100 meters across and the coma is never larger than the Sun
    d. The smallest comet is at least a kilometer and the coma can be larger than the Sun
    e. Some are tens of kilometers across and the coma can be larger than the Sun

40. According to the first passage, what does the name "single apparition comets" mean?
    a. They only appear during the part of their orbit that is nearer to the Sun.
    b. They stay in the solar system even though they are only apparent once.
    c. Their orbital periods are so long they only appear once across millennia.
    d. They only remain in the solar system long enough to pass the Sun once.
    e. They only appear once every 200 years.

Section 3: Verbal

Synonyms

Directions: Select the one word whose meaning is closest to the word in capital letters.

1. ENTHRALL
   a. bizarre
   b. devote
   c. extreme
   d. fascinate
   e. weary

2. COWARD
   a. boor
   b. brave
   c. gutless
   d. judge
   e. hero

3. NOVICE
   a. beginner
   b. expert
   c. naught
   d. nurse
   e. veteran

4. TEMPERATE
   a. extreme
   b. lenient
   c. moderate
   d. taut
   e. disagreeable

5. AUTHENTIC
   a. colorful
   b. flimsy
   c. genuine
   d. laughable
   e. invalid

6. SALVAGE
   a. bless
   b. recover
   c. slobber
   d. swagger
   e. injure

7. VERNACULAR
   a. ballad
   b. language
   c. poison
   d. silence
   e. formal

8. ATTEST
   a. accommodate
   b. bewitch
   c. heed
   d. vouch
   e. disprove

9. DERELICT
   a. abandoned
   b. corrupted
   c. depressed
   d. dispirited
   e. improved

10. ORDAIN
   a. adorn
   b. arrange
   c. command
   d. create
   e. neglect

11. HAUGHTY
   a. arrogant
   b. bitter
   c. obscure
   d. perilous
   e. humble

12. LASPE
   a. award
   b. error
   c. margin
   d. prank
   e. accurate

13. NAUSEATE
   a. annoy
   b. crave
   c. repulse
   d. rival
   e. attract

14. PALTRY
    a. cheap
    b. valuable
    c. peaceful
    d. severely
    e. plenty

15. REFINED
    a. aromatic
    b. blatant
    c. cultured
    d. frightened
    e. rough

16. VIRTUAL
    a. potent
    b. real
    c. simulated
    d. visible
    e. authentic

17. LOATHE
    a. charge
    b. exist
    c. fear
    d. hate
    e. commend

18. MIMIC
    a. curtail
    b. delve
    c. imitate
    d. recall
    e. deviate

19. BRITTLE
    a. broad
    b. fragile
    c. radical
    d. smooth
    e. flexible

20. WRETCHED
    a. absorbed
    b. awry
    c. miserable
    d. wicked
    e. lively

21. FALLIBLE
    a. certain
    b. infallible
    c. precise
    d. careful
    e. imperfect

22. ANGUISH
    a. loneliness
    b. confusion
    c. anger
    d. sorrow
    e. relief

23. VOLATILE
    a. firm
    b. calm
    c. predictable
    d. masked
    e. unstable

24. PALLID
    a. healthy
    b. sickly
    c. rosy
    d. deep
    e. glowing

25. DEMURE
    a. forward
    b. outgoing
    c. modest
    d. sociable
    e. bold

26. ADHERE
    a. unfasten
    b. revere
    c. loose
    d. convince
    e. unite

27. SOILED
    a. dirty
    b. sullen
    c. sultry
    d. dainty
    e. rich

28. PLIABLE
   a. fragile
   b. contrary
   c. rigid
   d. light
   e. spongy

29. DISDAIN
   a. favor
   b. fancy
   c. calculate
   d. scorn
   e. respect

30. STOIC
   a. bored
   b. tolerant
   c. grumble
   d. stammer
   e. impatient

Analogies

Directions: For each of the following questions, you will find terms and five answer choices designated a, b, c, d, and e. Select the one answer choice that best completes the analogy.

31. Punishment is to reprimand as impetuous is to
   a. cautious
   b. considerate
   c. hasty
   d. meticulous
   e. poor

32. Cue is to queue as
   a. incessant is to relentless
   b. joule is to jewel
   c. penultimate is to ultimate
   d. redress is to transgress
   e. solve is to revolve

33. Frog is to amphibian as hydrogen is to
   a. aerospace
   b. element
   c. galaxy
   d. instrumental
   e. seismograph

34. Light is to hologram as film is to
    a. aesthetic
    b. panoramic
    c. photographer
    d. transistor
    e. video camera

35. Superficial is to mature as
    a. approach is to reproach
    b. beguile is to deceive
    c. exorbitant is to excess
    d. noxious is to toxic
    e. submissive is to defiant

36. Innovation is to prodigy as
    a. editorial is to epic
    b. extract is to illusionist
    c. manuscript is to composer
    d. office is to faculty
    e. painting is to narrator

37. Rubber is to pliable as
    a. dream is to reality
    b. legacy is to immutable
    c. luck is to serendipity
    d. psychopath is to medicine
    e. rift is to solid

38. Kayak is to quest as
    a. antibiotic is to sneeze
    b. cloister is to party
    c. intercom is to communication
    d. memoir is to personal
    e. prudence is to foresight

39. Particle is to remnant as
    a. ameliorate is to alleviate
    b. irreverent is to religious
    c. indifference is to remorse
    d. sanguine is to pessimistic
    e. sedentary is to energetic

40. Cardiologist is to specialist as
    a. artifact is to journey
    b. crusade is to amoral
    c. kiwi is to vitamin
    d. parable is to fiction
    e. tribulation is to adversity

41. Politician is to policy as
    a. coach is to extrovert
    b. critic is to synopsis
    c. emissary is to dramatization
    d. police is to illegal
    e. spendthrift is to discipline

42. Error is to iniquity as
    a. cliché is to frivolous
    b. compassion is to forgiveness
    c. fragment is to whole
    d. lengthy is to transient
    e. wave is to tsunami

43. Gorilla is to guerilla as
    a. adroit is to incompetent
    b. enigma is to mystery
    c. lurch is to perch
    d. pseudonym is to prestige
    e. sign is to sine

44. Apathy is to persistence as
    a. anecdote is to narrative
    b. fatuous is to dense
    c. pervasive is to ubiquitous
    d. profuse is to sparse
    e. vale is to veil

45. Index is to book as elegy is to
    a. artifact
    b. audition
    c. equinox
    d. funeral
    e. penance

46. Tenet is to professor as
    a. exposition is to silence
    b. facsimile is to replica
    c. parody is to comedian
    d. pollen is to bee
    e. terrarium is to athlete

47. Underdog is to audacious as conspirator is to
    a. altruistic
    b. elusive
    c. illegible
    d. passive
    e. relic

48. Marshal is to martial as
    a. delude is to mislead
    b. earn is to urn
    c. lithe is to tithe
    d. ornate is to plain
    e. repel is to impel

49. Dollar is to salary as
    a. antihero is to prodigious
    b. festival is to decadence
    c. sprinter is to speedster
    d. tear is to melancholy
    e. wheel is to vehicle

50. Intermission is to drama as plant is to
    a. compliment
    b. constellation
    c. habitat
    d. memorabilia
    e. metropolitan

51. Copious is to extensive as
    a. amiss is to proper
    b. dubious is to undoubted
    c. epitome is to felicity
    d. resilient is to supple
    e. supreme is to paramount

52. Antagonist is to fiction as
    a. admonition is to forewarning
    b. marriage is to fidelity
    c. journal is to database
    d. mural is to iconic
    e. protagonist is to hero

53. Novella is to brief as
    a. computer is to microscopic
    b. dorm is to resilient
    c. infant is to naïve
    d. master is to unkempt
    e. star is to monitor

54. Jog is to marathon as hypothesis is to
    a. discovery
    b. forgery
    c. irate
    d. punishment
    e. surreal

55. Opinion is to connoisseur as
    a. hybrid is to innovator
    b. itinerary is to plan
    c. montage is to scientist
    d. riot is to heat
    e. season is to farmer

56. Insight is to decision as
    a. advocate is to defend
    b. conjecture is to truth
    c. guide is to misled
    d. ignition is to fuel
    e. neighbor is to fence

57. Antipathy is to sympathy as convivial is to
    a. avarice
    b. gloomy
    c. harmonious
    d. sociable
    e. wary

58. Espionage is to discreet as kindling is to
    a. grotesque
    b. majestic
    c. novelty
    d. ominous
    e. suave

59. Benediction is to ceremony as
    a. aroma is to odor
    b. landmark is to city
    c. introvert is to friend
    d. milestone is to suburb
    e. relationship is to personality

60. Interjection is to attorney as
    a. claim is to rejection
    b. insinuation is to judge
    c. money is to auction
    d. veil is to wedding
    e. voucher is to redeemer

Section 4: Quantitative

1. On his last math test, Sam got 2 questions correct for every 3 questions he missed. If the test had a total of 60 questions, how many questions did Sam answer correctly?
  a. 12
  b. 24
  c. 36
  d. 40
  e. 60

2. Solve $(3x + 1)(7x + 10)$
  a. $12x^2 + 17x + 10$
  b. $21x^2 + 37x + 10$
  c. $21x^2 + 23x + 10$
  d. $21x^2 + 37x + 9$
  e. $10x^2 + 21x + 11$

3. In the figure below, lines a and b are parallel. Find the value of x.

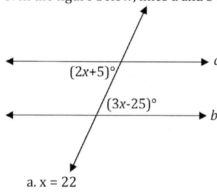

  a. $x = 22$
  b. $x = 30$
  c. $x = 40$
  d. $x = 55$
  e. $x = 65$

4. Joseph purchased 12 pounds of peaches at 80 cents per pound. He calculated the total amount as 12 x $0.80. = $9.60. Another method Joseph could have used to calculate the total cost of the peaches is:
  a. (10 x $0.80) + (2 x $0.80)
  b. (12 x $0.40) + (2 x $0.80)
  c. (12 x $0.20) + (12 x $0.20)
  d. (2 x $0.80) + (10 x $0.40)
  e. (10 x $0.80) + (2 x $0.40)

5. Joshua has to earn more than 92 points on the state test in order to qualify for an academic scholarship. Each question is worth 4 points, and the test has a total of 30 questions. Let x represent the number of test questions.

Which of the following inequalities can be solved to determine the number of questions Joshua must answer correctly?
    a. $4x < 30$
    b. $4x < 92$
    c. $4x > 30$
    d. $x > 30$
    e. $4x > 92$

6. If $\frac{4}{x-3} - \frac{2}{x} = 1$, then $x = ?$
    a. -6
    b. -1
    c. -6 or -1
    d. -1 or 6
    e. 6 or 1

7. The histogram below represents the overall GRE scores for a sample of college students. Which of the following is a true statement?

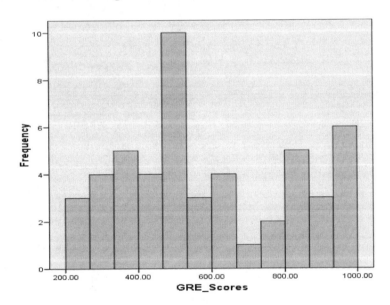

    a. The range of GRE scores is approximately 600
    b. The average GRE score is 750
    c. The median GRE score is approximately 500
    d. The fewest number of college students had an approximate score of 800
    e. The median GRE score is approximately 300.

8. If $a \neq 0$, then $12a^2b \div 3a = ?$
    a. $4a$
    b. $4b$
    c. $4ab$
    d. $9b^2$
    e. $9ab$

9. If the square of twice the sum of x and three is equal to the product of twenty-four and x, which of these is a possible value of x?
    a. $6 + 3\sqrt{2}$
    b. $\frac{3}{2}$
    c. $-3i$
    d. -3
    e. -9

10. What statement best describes the rate of change?

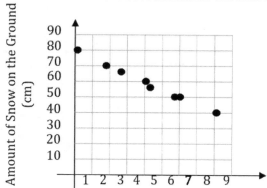

Number of Days
    a. Every day, the snow melts 10 centimeters.
    b. Every day, the snow melts 5 centimeters.
    c. Every day, the snow increases by 10 centimeters.
    d. Every day, the snow increases by 5 centimeters.
    e. None of the above.

11. What is the expected value of drawing a card from a deck when the cards are labeled 1 – 5?
    a. 1.5
    b. 2
    c. 2.5
    d. 3
    e. 3.5

12. Which of the following represents the expected value of the number of tails Adam will get after tossing a coin 6 times?
    a. 2
    b. 3
    c. 6
    d. 9
    e. 12

13. Based on the figure below, if $BG = 6x - 4$ and $GD = 2x + 8$, what is the length of $\overline{GD}$?

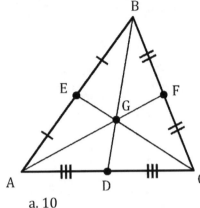

    a. 10
    b. 14
    c. 28
    d. 34
    e. 56

14. Matthew has to earn more than 96 points on his high school entrance exam in order to be eligible for varsity sports. Each question is worth 3 points, and the test has a total of 40 questions. Let x represent the number of test questions.

How many questions can Matthew answer incorrectly and still qualify for varsity sports?
    a. $x < 8$
    b. $x > 8$
    c. $x > 32$
    d. $0 < x \leq 8$
    e. $0 \leq x < 8$

15. A box in the form of a rectangular solid has a square base of 5 feet in length, a width of 5 feet, and a height of h feet. If the volume of the rectangular solid is 200 cubic feet, which of the following equations may be used to find h?
    a. 5h = 200
    b. 5h² = 200
    c. 25h = 200
    d. h = 200 ÷ 5
    e. 10h = 200

16. Robert is planning to drive 1,800 miles on a cross-country trip. If his car gets 30 miles to the gallon, and his tank holds 12 gallons of gas, how many tanks of gas will he need to complete the trip?

a. 3 tanks of gas
b. 5 tanks of gas
c. 10 tanks of gas
d. 30 tanks of gas
e. 60 tanks of gas

17. Which line appears to have a slope of 2?

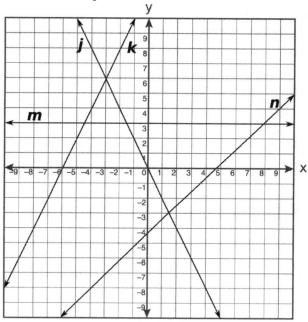

a. Line j
b. Line k
c. Line m
d. Line n
e. None of the lines

18. Three quarters of the students running a 100-yard race finished with an average time of 16 seconds. The remaining 25% of students finished with an average time of 12 seconds. What was the average time overall?
a. 13 seconds
b. 14 seconds
c. 15 seconds
d. 16 seconds
e. 20 seconds

19. A bag contains 8 red marbles, 3 blue marbles, and 4 green marbles. What is the probability Carlos draws a red marble, does not replace it, and then draws another red marble?

a. $\frac{2}{15}$

b. $\frac{4}{15}$

c. $\frac{64}{225}$

d. $\frac{32}{105}$

e. $\frac{15}{29}$

20. If $\sqrt{3x - 2} = x - 2$, then $x = ?$

a. 1
b. 6
c. −1 or 6
d. 1 or 6
e. None of the above

21. If $7\sqrt{x} + 16 = 79$, what is the value of x?

a. 6
b. 9
c. 27
d. 46
e. 81

22. Which of the following is equivalent to $27x^3 + y^3$?

a. $(3x + y)(3x + y)(3x + y)$
b. $(3x + y)(9x^2 - 3xy + y^2)$
c. $(3x - y)(9x^2 + 3xy + y^2)$
d. $(3x - y)(9x^2 + 9xy + y^2)$
e. $(3x + y)(9x^2 - 3xy - y^2)$

23. On a road map, $\frac{1}{4}$ inch represents 8 miles of actual road distance. The towns of Dinuba and Clovis are measured to be $2\frac{1}{8}$ inches apart on the map. What is the actual distance, in miles, between the two towns?

a. 32
b. 40
c. 60
d. 68
e. 76

24. In the figure below, $\triangle JKL$ is dilated to the image $\triangle J'K'L'$.

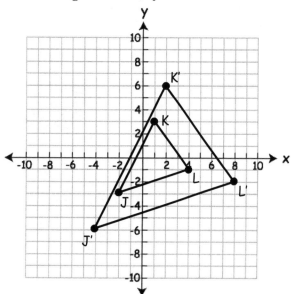

What is the scale factor of the dilation?

   a. $\frac{1}{3}$

   b. $\frac{1}{2}$

   c. $\frac{3}{4}$

   d. 2

   e. 3

25. In the figure shown here, the arc $\overset{\frown}{AB}$ is 4 meters long, and the total perimeter of the circle is 48 meters. Which of the following best represents the measure of $\angle AOB$, which subtends arc $\overset{\frown}{AB}$?

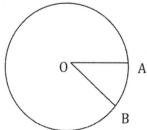

   a. 15 degrees
   b. 30 degrees
   c. 45 degrees
   d. 55 degrees
   e. 60 degrees

Answers and Explanations

Section 1: Quantitative

1. B: To solve, first subtract Jerry's weight from the total permitted: 800-200 = 600. Divide 600 by 4 (the four pieces of equipment) to get 150, the average weight.

2. C: The correct answer is $3000. Besides the $600 he has remaining, Chan has paid out a total of 80% (30% + 20% +20%+10%) of his bonus for the expenses described in the question. Therefore, the $600 represents the remaining 20%. To determine his total bonus, solve $\frac{100}{20} \times 600 = 3000$.

3. A: If the ratio of pennies to nickels is 2:6, the ratio of the pennies to the combined coins is 2:2+6, or 2:8. This is $\frac{1}{4}$ or, expressed as a percentage, 25%.

4. D: The literal equation may be solved for x by first subtracting b from both sides of the equation. Doing so gives $ax = c - b$. Dividing both sides of the equation by a gives $x = \frac{c-b}{a}$.

5. A: There are 4 members of the first set and 4 members of the second set, so there are 4(4) = 16 possible products for cd. cd is odd only when both c and d are odd. There are 2 odd numbers in the first set and two in the second set, so 2(2) = 4 products are odd and the probability cd is odd is 4/16 or 1/4.

6. C: The given equations form a system of linear equations. Since the first equation is already given in terms of x, it will be easier to solve it using the substitution method. Start by substituting $2y - 3$ for x in the second equation:

$$2x + \frac{1}{2}y = 3$$

$$2(2y - 3) + \frac{1}{2}y = 3$$

Next, solve the resulting equation for y. Distribute the 2 and then combine like y-terms in the result:

$$4y - 6 + \frac{1}{2}y = 3$$

$$\frac{9}{2}y - 6 = 3$$

Finally, isolate the variable y by adding 6 to both sides and then dividing both sides by the coefficient of y, which is $\frac{9}{2}$ (or, equivalently, multiply by 2 and divide by 9):

$$\frac{9}{2}y = 9$$

$$y = 2$$

7. B: Add the 14 blue, 6 red, 12 green and 8 purple buttons to get a total of 40 buttons. If 25 buttons are removed, there are 15 buttons remaining in the bag. The chance of drawing a

red button is now $\frac{1}{3}$. So, you divide 15 into thirds to get 5 red buttons remaining in the bag. The original total of red buttons was 6; so 6 – 5 = 1: one red button was removed, choice (B).

8. E: The sides of a triangle must all be greater than zero. The sum of the lengths of the two shorter sides must be greater than the length of the third side. Since we are looking for the minimum value of the perimeter, assume the longer of the two given sides, which is 6, is the longest side of the triangle. Then the third side must be greater than 6 – 4 = 2. Since we are told the sides are all integral numbers, the last side must be 3 units in length. Thus, the minimum length for the perimeter is 4+6+3 = 13 units.

9. C: A set of six numbers with an average of 4 must have a collective sum of 24. The two numbers that average 2 will add up to 4, so the remaining numbers must add up to 20. The average of these four numbers can be calculated: 20/4 = 5.

10. A: This table shows the numbers of coins added to the first few squares and the equivalent powers of 2:

Square	1	2	3	4
Coins	1	2	4	8
Power of 2	2^0	2^1	2^2	2^3

In this series, the number of coins on each is the consecutive powers of 2. The reason is that the number doubles with each consecutive square. However, the series of powers begins with 0 for the first square. For the 64th square, the number of coins will be 2^{63}.

11. D: First establish a variable, s, for the length of the smaller square. Since the larger square is 3 feet longer than the smaller one, its length is $s + 3$. Given that the difference between the areas of the two squares is 75, and the area of any square is equal to its side lengths squared, the following equation can be established:

$$(s + 3)^2 - s^2 = 75$$

Simplify the left side of the equation:
$$(s + 3)^2 - s^2 = 75$$
$$(s + 3)(s + 3) - s^2 = 75$$
$$s^2 + 6s + 9 - s^2 = 75$$
$$6s + 9 = 75$$

Isolate the variable and divide both sides by its coefficient to solve for s:
$$6s = 66$$
$$s = 11$$

Therefore, the length of the smaller square is 11 feet.

12. A: Setting the cost of shipping equal to the amount received gives us the equation $3,000 + 100x = 400x$. Subtract 100x from both sides to get $3,000 = 300x$, then divide both sides by 300 to see that $x = 10$.

13. B: $\frac{x}{8}$ and $\frac{y}{4}$ both equal 4. Now, $\frac{x}{8}=4$, and $x = 8 \times 4 = 32$.

Then, $\frac{y}{4} = 4$. So, $y = 4 \times 4 = 16$

$x - y = 32 - 16 = 16$

14. A: To solve, you will need to move the decimal 4 places. Since the scientific notation had a negative power of 10, move the decimal left. If the power of 10 had been positive, you would have needed to move it to the right. In this problem, solve as follows:
7.4 x 10⁻⁴
7.4 x 1/10,000
7.4 x 0.0001
0.00074

15. E: The area of the squares, whose side lengths are the legs of the triangles, are a^2 and b^2, or in this example, 9 squares and 9 squares. The area of the square whose side lengths are equal to the hypotenuse of the right triangle is c^2. If the whole squares, and half squares, in the grid are summed, the area of the square with side length c is 18 squares. The area of the squares whose side lengths are the legs of the triangles, summed, equals the area of the square whose side lengths are the hypotenuse of the triangle.
9 squares + 9 squares = 18 squares, or $a^2 + b^2 = c^2$

16. A: Put this into an algebraic equation:
5 + 6x = 77
Subtract 5 from both sides:
6x = 72
Divide both sides by 6 to get x = 12

17. C: Multiply the first numbers in each of the parentheses to get 6, and add the exponents of the tens. $(2 \times 10^5) \times (3 \times 10^4) = 2 \times 3 \times 10^{5+4} = 6 \times 10^9$.

18. D: When the factors, $(x - 4)$ and $(x + 7)$ are multiplied, the x-terms sum to $3x$ and the constants produce a product of −28.

19. B: Solve the inequality by changing the inequality sign to an equal sign and solve the resulting equation by factoring the left side:

$$x^2 - 7x + 10 = 0$$
$$(x-2)(x-5) = 0$$
$$x - 2 = 0 \quad \text{or} \quad x - 5 = 0$$
$$x = 2 \qquad\qquad x = 5$$

Since the original inequality sign was a greater-than-or-equal-to sign (rather than just a greater-than sign), the solution set will include $x = 2$ and $x = 5$.

These two solutions divide the number line into three distinct regions: $x < 2$, $2 < x < 5$, and $x > 5$. To see which regions are in the solution set, pick one test value from each region and substitute it in the original inequality. If the result is a true inequality, then the whole region is part of the solution set. Otherwise, the whole region is not part in the solution set:

Region	Test Value	$x^2 - 7x + 10 \geq 0$	Conclusion
$x < 2$	0	$(0)^2 - 7(0) + 10 \geq 0$ $7 \geq 0$	Part of the solution set
$2 < x < 5$	3	$(3)^2 - 7(3) + 10 \geq 0$ $9 - 21 + 10 \geq 0$ $-2 \geq 0$	Not part of the solution set
$x > 5$	6	$(6)^2 - 7(6) + 10 \geq 0$ $36 - 42 + 10 \geq 0$ $4 \geq 0$	Part of the solution set

Therefore, the solution set is $x \leq 2$ or $x \geq 5$.

20. C: First write Equation A in slope-intercept form: $y = mx + b$ where m is the slope and b is the y-intercept.
$$5y - 100x = 25$$
$$5y = 100x + 25$$
$$y = 20x + 5$$
Based on the slope-intercept form of Equation A, the slope, m = 20 and the y-intercept, b = 5.

21. B: The chart indicates that 40% of the total recycled material is paper. Since 50,000 tons of material are recycled every month, the total amount of paper will be 40% of 50,000 tons, or $\frac{40}{100} \times 50{,}000 = 20{,}000$ tons.

22. C: The volume of the box is the product of $\sqrt{3}$, $2\sqrt{5}$, and 4. To multiply two or more square root radicals, multiply the coefficients and then multiply the radicands:
$$\sqrt{3} \times 2\sqrt{5} \times 4 = 2\sqrt{15} \times 4$$
$$= 8\sqrt{15}$$

23. C: Because both expressions share the factor 10^3, we can simply factor and add the ones places. $(8 \times 10^3) + (1 \times 10^3) = (1 + 8)(10^3) = 9 \times 10^3$.

24. B: The y-intercept of the line is $(0, -1)$. Another point on the line is $(1,0)$. Slope is the vertical change over horizontal change which is $\frac{1}{1} = 1$. Plugging this information into the slope-intercept form $y = mx + b$, the equation is $y = x - 1$.

25. E: When the dress is marked down by 20%, the cost of the dress is 80% of its original price; thus, the reduced price of the dress can be written as $\frac{80}{100}x$, or $\frac{4}{5}x$, where x is the original price. When discounted an extra 25%, the dress costs 75% of the reduced price, or $\frac{75}{100}\left(\frac{4}{5}x\right)$, or $\frac{3}{4}\left(\frac{4}{5}x\right)$, which simplifies to $\frac{3}{5}x$. So the final price of the dress is three-fifths of the original price.

Section 2: Reading Comprehension

1. B: There is no indication in the passage that the Bennets are interested in becoming friends with Mr. Bingley (choice A), that Mr. Bingley would be a valuable business connection (choice C), that Mr. Bingley has any prior knowledge of the Bennet daughters (choice D), or that Mr. Bingley has an interest in acquiring more property beyond Netherfiled Park (choice E). Mrs. Bennet tells her husband that a new neighbor is moving in: "Mrs. Long says that Netherfield is taken by a young man of large fortune." Mrs. Bennet is sure he will make an excellent husband for one of her daughters: "You must know that I am thinking of his marrying one of them."

2. A: Mrs. Bennet is quite excited and feels that Mr. Bingley is likely to marry one of her daughters. She tells her husband that Mr. Bingley is a "single man of large fortune; four or five thousand a year. What a fine thing for our girls!"

3. B: Mrs. Bennet is annoyed and fed up with her husband's seeming indifference to Mr. Bingley: "'My dear Mr. Bennet,' replied his wife, 'how can you be so tiresome!'"

4. A: "It is a truth universally acknowledged" means that something is understood to be true by the general public.

5. E: Mr. Bennet is facetiously asking if the idea of marriage (particularly to one of his own daughters) was Mr. Bingley's intention when he agreed to rent Netherfield Park.

6. B: The passage discusses Helen Keller's life beginning with her birth and continuing on into her adulthood.

7. E: The passage does mention that Helen graduated from Radcliffe College (choice A), and the passage does tell about Anne's role as Helen's teacher (choice B), but the passage as a whole does not focus on Helen's time at college or Anne's life outside of her role as teacher. The passage does not mention services available for the deaf and blind (choice C). The passage does tell about Helen Keller's life.

8. C: The second paragraph explains why Anne Sullivan was crucial to Helen's life, and the third paragraph elaborates on how Anne helped Helen succeed.

9. C: The author's use of the phrase "Helen learned at an incredible rate" and the word "remarkable" to describe Helen's life are two examples of the author's admiration.

10. D: Although all of the answer choices represent major events in Helen's life, the passage specifies that the advent of Anne Sullivan was the turning point in Helen's life when she began to learn to communicate with other people. "All of that began to change in March 1887 when Anne Sullivan came to live with the Kellers and be Helen's teacher. Anne taught Helen to communicate by forming letters with her fingers held in another person's hand."

11. A: The passage does not indicate that Helen's parents were jealous of Anne (choice B), glad to give Anne responsibility for Helen (choice C), had any preference in their daughter's choice of a college (choice D), or wished that they had asked for Mrs. Sullivan's help at an earlier time (choice E). The passage does say that Helen's parents loved her and that they brought Anne to their home to be Helen's teacher. This implies that they were frustrated by their own inability to help Helen and were looking for someone who could help.

12. C: The passage describes several distinctive features of annelid anatomy and tells how some of them differ from other worms.

13. E: The text gives the example of feet specializing into grasping organs to illustrate this evolutionary advantage of segmental plasticity.

14. C: The text defines metemeres as segments, and discusses segmentation as the distinguishing feature of the phylum.

15. D: The paragraph tells us that annelids can live in salt or fresh water and on land, and then gives examples.

16. D: The author compares (A) annelids and nematodes as both having a fluid-filled internal *coelum* or cavity separating the body wall and gut, and both having this cavity involved in their locomotion. The author also contrasts (B) the two phyla in that annelids develop this cavity much later during both embryonic growth and ("presumably") evolutionary progress. Hence both comparison and contrast (D) relationships are established, meaning (C) and (E) are incorrect.

17. B: After the initial topic sentence, the first paragraph discusses metameric segmentation as a distinctive feature of annelids. The second paragraph discusses annelid body parts, i.e., the gut, body wall, and *coelum*, including their functions, development, and differences and similarities of the latter between annelids and nematodes. The third paragraph discusses annelid body systems, including excretory, circulatory, respiratory, and nervous. The fourth and final paragraph includes annelid habitat adaptations and names three well-known types.

18. D: Hughes uses (extended) metaphor by describing the concrete presence of an animal, a fox, to represent the abstract entity of an inspiration for the writer to produce poetry. From beyond the blank window, starless sky, and dark forest, the fox, as a totem for the writer's imagination, approaches from without to inspire, its pawprints in the snow

- 123 -

symbolizing print appearing on the blank page. Foreshadowing (A) is the literary device of hinting earlier in a work at something that will become more apparent later. Irony (B) is the device of creating a discrepancy between what is expected and what really occurs (verbal, dramatic, or situational irony). Hughes's work is notable for NOT including any overused expressions known as clichés (C). Finally, there is no significant literary or historical reference for an allusion (E).

19. C: The poem describes how the poet is inspired to write, using the fox to embody the thought that enters the poet's mind (hence the title The Thought-Fox). The fox's natural actions (A) are thus symbolic rather than literal. The poet is not inspired by nature (B); in this poem, he uses an element of nature (the fox) to represent the thought that he receives and writes. The fox's entering "the head" is not a literal attack (D) but a symbolic representation of having or getting that thought. The poet does not work for a print shop (E), instead he is writing down his ideas of inspiration.

20. E: The poet's passivity and lack of control over the thought, or content, of his writing can be interpreted from Hughes's separation of the thought, which does not arise from within his head, but approaches symbolically in the form of a fox from outside of his head, his body, and even his house. This separation is emphasized by the description of the Thought-Fox as "Coming about its own business." The poet as passive recipient is further shown in the last stanza, where the fox "...enters the dark hole of the head." This passivity of the artist is further reflected in the last line, "The page is printed," wherein Hughes uses the passive voice to represent the thought/writing process, rather than saying that he himself prints the page.

21. B: Lincoln begins this speech by discussing the founding of the U.S. and what the original purpose of the U.S. was. Then, he goes on to talk about how the U.S. is currently engaged in a war intended to fracture the nation, and he states that the battle being discussed was one large tragedy that came out of the war. Next, Lincoln says that his speech and even the memorial itself can't truly honor those who died, and that it's up to those who survived to continue the fight to ensure the nation does not break apart. Answer B best communicates this message.

22. E: The sentence in which this phrase is found is: The world will little note, nor long remember, what we say here, but can never forget what they did here. In this context, the phrase "the world will little note" means that no one outside of those in attendance or possibly those outside the country will pay attention to the speech or the ceremony. This eliminates all of the answer choices except E.

23. A: The ideals of the revolution are addressed in the first paragraph: Four score and seven years ago our fathers brought forth, upon this continent, a new nation, conceived in Liberty, and dedicated to the proposition that all men are created equal. This introduces the point that Lincoln is trying to make about the battle at hand and the war as a whole: the Civil War is threatening the ideas upon which the nation was created.

24. C: There is a comparison between the ideas of the Revolution and the Civil War in this speech. To facilitate understanding of this comparison, Lincoln has to set the stage by telling his audience about the past event he is referencing. This establishes the context of his message.

25. A: This line directly references the idea in the previous paragraph, which is that the U.S. is a nation that was created to ensure liberty and equality. This sentence talks about how the Civil War is testing whether or not a nation that was created to ensure liberty and equality can really survive.

26. B: When President Lincoln argues that the people who died at Gettysburg did not die in vain, he asserts that their passing was not frivolous or unimportant or meaningless.

27. D: This information is all given in the second paragraph.

28. C: In the fourth paragraph, the author states that the transient nature of relationships based solely on shared interests is keeping us "socially busy without building the lasting relationships and communities that we want."

29. B: The author lists urban sprawl, long work hours, and devotion to television and the internet as causes of problems for American communities.

30. B: This is the only one of the answer choices that is not listed in the fourth paragraph as suggestions put forth by the Harvard University study.

31. E: The author states in the fourth paragraph that Harvard University School of Government put forth 150 suggestions for increasing social capital.

32. D: Foreshadowing is the best choice. Choice (A), first person point of view, does not answer the question and is incorrect because the story is told from the third person point of view. Choice (B) is incorrect because "hyperbole" generally refers to unrealistic exaggeration, but the imagery in this passage is realistic, even if it does describe extreme conditions. Choice (C), onomatopoeia, is incorrect because the passage contains no words like "cluck" or "quack" that sound like what they describe. Choice (E), symbolism, does not adequately answer the question posed.

33. D: Choice (E) is close to being the answer, but Choice (D) is the best answer because the narrator can enter the consciousness of both the man and the dog, making it third person omniscient. Choices (A) and (B) can be ruled out because the narrator does not use the pronouns "I" or "we." Choice (C) does not seem likely because the passage gives us no reason to believe that the narrator's account of this information cannot be trusted.

34. A: Choice A offers the best interpretation. The passage refers to immortality and man's place in the universe; the man does not have the imagination to contemplate such issues, and he does not seem to realize the frailty of humans on the planet. Choices (B), (C), and (E) contradict or misinterpret the meaning of the passage. Choice (D) is not really implied by the passage; in fact, the dog's instincts make it seem more intelligent than the man in a certain sense.

35. C: It can be supported by the following quotation: "[The dog's] instinct told it a truer tale than was told to the man by the man's judgment." Choice (A) may sound possible, but it does not really capture the narrator's main point of comparison. Choice (B) can be contradicted by the following quotation: "In its brain there was no sharp consciousness of a condition of very cold such as was in the man's brain." Choices (D) and (E) can also be contradicted by the preceding quotation.

36. B: The second sentence in the passage notes that comets are distinguishable from asteroids by the presence of comas or tails.

37. C: The third paragraph notes that there are over 3,500 known comets. It also notes that this represents only a small portion of those in existence.

38. C: The second paragraph notes that because they have low mass, they don't become spherical and have irregular shapes.

39. E: The second paragraph notes that some comets may be tens of kilometers across. It also notes that comas may be larger than the sun.

40. D: The passage defines single apparition comets as those whose trajectories make them pass the Sun once and then exit our solar system permanently. It also describes most comets as having oval orbits wherein they are nearer to the Sun during part of their orbit, and then move farther away from the Sun *within the solar system* for the rest of the orbit; hence (a) is incorrect. While single apparition comets are only apparent once, they are NOT still in the solar system (b). The passage defines short and long orbital periods, but does not include long orbital periods in that definition (c).

Section 3: Verbal

1. D: To enthrall is to fascinate or mesmerize.

2. C: A coward is someone who is gutless or lacks courage when facing danger.

3. A: A novice is someone who is new to the circumstances, or the person is a beginner.

4. C: Temperate means to be moderate or restrained.

5. C: Something authentic is genuine or true.

6. B: To salvage something is to save or recover it from wreckage, destruction, or loss.

7. B: Vernacular is the speech or language of a place.

8. D: To attest is to vouch for or to certify.

9. A: Derelict means to be neglected or abandoned, e.g., "a derelict old home."

10. C: To ordain is to order or command.

11. A: To be haughty is to be proud or arrogant.

12. B: A lapse is an error or mistake, e.g., "a lapse of memory."

13. C: To nauseate is to disgust or repulse.

14. A: Something paltry is cheap, base, or common.

15. C: To be refined is to be cultured and well-bred.

16. C: Virtual means to be simulated, especially as related to computer software.

17. D: To loathe is to hate or abhor.

18. C: When you mimic, you imitate or copy someone or something.

19. B: Something brittle is fragile and easily damaged or destroyed.

20. C: Wretched means miserable or woeful.

21. E: A fallible person or object is one that is faulty or imperfect.

22. D: Somebody who is experiencing or feeling anguish is experiencing sorrow or sadness.

23. E: A volatile situation or person is one that is unstable or changeable.

24. B: A person who is said to be pallid is feeble or sickly.

25. C: An individual who is described as demure is someone who is modest or timid.

26. E: When someone is told that they need to adhere to the group, they are being asked to become attached or united with the others of their group.

27. A: Something that is soiled is stained or dirty. When somebody says their clothing is soiled, it is the same as saying that their clothing is dirty.

28. E: An object that is pliable is understood to be very flexible or spongy.

29. D: When you have disdain for something or someone, you despise or scorn that person or thing.

30. B: A stoic is an individual that is very tolerant, or one who can suffer a great deal without raising a complaint.

31. C: This analogy focuses on synonyms. *Reprimand* and *punishment* are close synonyms. *Impetuous* is a sudden or impulsive action with little or no thoughtful planning. So, the best choice is *hasty* which means rapid or very quick.

32. B: This analogy focuses on homonyms. *Cue* and *queue* have different spellings, but they sound very similar. The best answer choice of *joule* and *jewel* also has different spellings with similar pronunciations.

33. B: The category of amphibians contains frogs. The order of this analogy begins with something that is specific and moves to the general category. Since you are given the specific item of *hydrogen*, then you are looking for the general category which would be choice B: *element*.

34. E: A *hologram* is an image that is made up of beams of *light* from a laser. So, we could say that the order of this analogy is a piece of a whole. The start of the next comparison is *film* which would be a piece of a *video camera*.

35. E: *Superficial* means shallow or lacking detail. M*ature* means complete development or ripe. So, this combination points to antonyms. The best answer choice is choice E which has the antonyms of *submissive* and *defiant*. *Submissive* means compliant or prone to submitting. *Defiant* means resisting opposition or disobedient.

36. C: The rare individual with insight into his or her craft at a very young age and makes startling *innovations* can receive the title of *prodigy*. The connection between these two words can be understood as a product being put together by a producer. Then, the best choice is the product of a *manuscript* (i.e., a document that is written by hand or has not been published) being produced by a *composer* (i.e., person who writes music).

37. B: *Rubber* material has the characteristic of being very flexible or *pliable*. So, the comparison to be made is how something or someone has a certain characteristic or attribute. The best choice is choice B as a characteristic of a *legacy* is its durability or *immutability*.

38. C: Among the many uses of a *kayak* is to depart on *quests*. The best choice is how an *intercom* is used to spread *communication*.

39. A: This analogy focuses on synonyms. *Particle* and *remnant* are close synonyms. *Ameliorate* means to improve, and *alleviate* means to lessen pain or trouble in an attempt to improve the situation. The other choices are antonyms.

40. D: A *cardiologist* is a doctor who focuses on the functions and diseases of the heart. This doctor is different than a general practice doctor because *cardiologists* are considered *specialists*. A *specialist* is a category of several kinds of doctors that includes dermatologists (focus on skin), immunologists (focus on immune system), neurologists (focus on nervous system), and many others. The best choice is how a *parable* (e.g., short story with a moral or religious teaching) stands among the many pieces of the category of *fiction*.

41. B: A *politician* is someone who has experience in government and normally is an elected official. A *policy* is a plan with general goals for a government that will influence decisions or actions in matters that are foreign or domestic. So, a *politician* is someone who would use *policy*. The comparison to be made is how a *critic* who can review books, television shows, movies, and many other things will also need to be able to write a *synopsis* (e.g., a summary or overview) of the work.

42. E: This analogy is a matter of degree as starting with something basic and escalating to something more significant. The question begins with *error* which is basic and general, and this is matched with *iniquity* which is a wicked act. So, the best choice is choice E which starts with a basic wave and escalates to a tsunami which is an incredibly high and large wave that can be the cause of destruction when meeting land.

43. E: This analogy focuses on homonyms. *Gorilla* and *guerilla* have different spellings, but they sound very similar. The best answer choice of *sign* and *sine* also has different spellings with similar pronunciations.

44. D: This analogy focuses on antonyms. *Apathy* and *persistence* are opposites as *apathy* means an absence of interest or feeling emotion, and *persistence* is a dedication to continue with an action despite opposition. *Profuse* means produced in large quantities, and *sparse* is an antonym as it means thin or existing in small quantities.

45. D: As a reference at the end of a *book*, an *index* may be provided that contains key terms or phrases with page numbers where those terms or phrases can be found. So, we can say that an *index* is a part to the whole of a *book*. The comparison involves an *elegy* which can be a song or a poem that expresses terrible sadness for the death of a person. This *elegy* would then be a part to the whole of a *funeral* service.

46. C: In a classroom or in research, a *professor* will speak on a topic or share his or her opinions that come from experience or study. Some of these opinions will come from the professor's *tenets* which are doctrines or principles that are held as being true. So, the comparison is one of a principle being produced by a *professor*. When you consider the options, the best choice is how a *parody* (e.g., imitation with comic intent) is produced by a *comedian*.

47. B: When a strong opponent competes against an unlikely challenger, we sometimes call the unlikely challenger an *underdog* who will face the incredible odds of defeating the strong opponent. An attribute or characteristic of an underdog can be their *audacious* (i.e., confident or bold) attitude. Now, a *conspirator* is a person who is participating in a plan that has some illegal intent. So, a conspirator has the characteristic of being *elusive* (i.e., easily escaping capture).

48. B: This analogy focuses on homonyms. *Marshal* and *martial* have different spellings, but they sound very similar. The best answer choice of *earn* and *urn* also has different spellings with similar pronunciations.

49. D: This analogy is a matter of degree as starting with something basic and escalating to something more significant. The question starts with a basic and general dollar which is escalated to a salary (i.e., a fixed amount of money that a person makes over a regular schedule). A *tear* is connected to sadness and weeping. So, a *tear* would be the basic or general start that escalates to the significant of being *melancholy*.

50. C: An *intermission* is a pause between acts of a play. Two common types of plays are *dramas* and comedies. So, we can determine that an *intermission* is a piece to the whole of a *drama*. Now, the comparison begins with *plant* as in vegetation. So, the best answer choice is *habitat* (i.e., the place where animal and plant life are naturally living) which fills the role of being the whole to the piece of *plant*.

51. D: This analogy focuses on synonyms. *Copious* (i.e., large in amount or number) and *extensive* (i.e., large in amount or size) are close synonyms. *Resilient* means flexible or able to recover or change after going through strain, and *supple* means able to fold or bend without much difficulty.

52. C: In fiction, you can find that many stories have both a protagonist and an *antagonist*. The protagonist is the person who is the main character of a story, and the *antagonist* is the person who is the opposing character to the protagonist. Now, an antagonist is a small piece to the whole of fiction. So, the best answer in the same order of piece to whole is *journal* to *database*. An example would be a peer-reviewed scientific journal that is found in an online research database.

53. C: A *novella* is a story with a number of pages that is less than a novel but is more than a short story. So, a certain characteristic of a *novella* is that it is *brief*. Then, you need to know which answer choice has the correct comparison for a characteristic. Among the choices, an *infant* being *naïve* (i.e., innocent) is the best option.

54. A: This analogy is a matter of degree as starting with something basic and escalating to something more significant. The question begins with *jog* which is basic and general, and this is matched with *marathon* which is a 26.2 mile race that takes several hours to complete. So, the best choice is choice A which starts with a basic *hypothesis* (i.e., educated guess) and escalates to a *discovery*.

55. A: *Connoisseurs* are critics or experts about their field or area of study who often lend their *opinions* to the general public. One could understand this as a product of an *opinion* that is produced by a *connoisseur*. Then, the comparison to be made is that a *hybrid* (i.e.,

- 130 -

combination or mixture) is produced by an *innovator* (i.e., a person who works on new ideas or methods).

56. A: When a *decision* needs to be made, some prefer to go with their instincts and others prefer to have wisdom or *insight* provided before making a commitment. So, one could say that *insight* is used to make *decisions*. Now, the correct comparison comes with an *advocate* (e.g., a lawyer) who *defends* someone or something against opposition.

57. B: This analogy focuses on antonyms. *Antipathy* and *sympathy* are opposites as *antipathy* means a strong feeling of opposition, and *sympathy* is the act of understanding another person's feeling or situation. You are given *convivial* which means sociable or cheerful, and you know that you are looking for the antonym of sociable and cheerful. So, *gloomy* means depressed or miserable, and this is the clear opposite to *convivial*.

58. D: *Espionage* is the service of spying on opposition in order to gain intelligence. So, the nature (or characteristic) of this task is easily understood to be *discreet* (i.e., tactful and cautious). The analogy continues with *kindling* which are the pieces of material used to start a fire. In many situations, a fire is characteristic of something tragic that is about to happen to someone or something. A name for this foreboding sense of tragedy can be *ominous*. In short, a characteristic of *kindling* is *ominous*.

59. B: A *benediction* is a prayer of blessing or expression of hope that is the final part of some religious services or general *ceremonies*. Since a *benediction* is a piece to the whole of a *ceremony*, you need to look for the choice that has a similar comparison. A *landmark* is a building or place in a town or *city* that is marked by historical significance and is sometimes officially recognized and preserved. So, the piece would be a *landmark*, and the whole would be a *city*.

60. E: While an *interjection* is commonly understood as one of the eight parts of speech, the term is also applicable to a statement that interrupts a situation or dialogue. An example could be a prosecutor that interrupts the dialogue between the defense attorney and a witness on the stand because he or she wants to make a plea to the judge. So, in this example an *interjection* is being used by an *attorney*. The best comparison comes with choice E as a *voucher* (i.e., coupon) needs to be redeemed (i.e., claimed) in order for the *redeemer* to receive the benefit of the *voucher*.

Section 4: Quantitative

1. B: The ratio of correct to incorrect answers is 2:3, giving a whole of 5. It takes 12 sets of 5 questions to total 60 questions. To determine how many correct answers Sam gave, multiply 2 by 12, for a total of 24.

2. B: Use the FOIL method (First, Outer, Inner, Last) to solve this equation:
(3x + 1) (7x + 10)
= (3x)(7x) + (3x)(10) + (1)(7x) + (1)(10)
= 21x² + 30x + 7x + 10
Combine like terms to get the answer:
21x² + 37x + 10

3. B: The listed angles are located in the alternate interior angles position. According to the Alternate Interior Angle Theorem, when a transversal cuts across parallel lines, the alternate interior angles are congruent. Since lines a and b are parallel, it means that $2x + 5 = 3x - 25$. After subtracting $2x$ from both sides and adding 25 to both sides, the equation simplifies as $30 = x$.

4. A: The answer is expanded to simplify the calculations. The total of Choice A is $8.00 + $1.60, which is the same as the total calculated in the problem.

5. E: In order to determine the number of questions Joshua must answer correctly, consider the number of points he must earn. Joshua will receive 4 points for each question he answers correctly, and x represents the number of questions. Therefore, Joshua will receive a total of 4x points for all the questions he answers correctly. Joshua must earn more than 92 points. Therefore, to determine the number of questions he must answer correctly, solve the inequality $4x > 92$.

6. D: To solve the equation, first get rid of the denominators by multiplying both sides of the equation by $x(x - 3)$ and simplifying the result:

$$\frac{4}{x-3} - \frac{2}{x} = 1$$

$$x(x-3)\left[\frac{4}{x-3} - \frac{2}{x}\right] = x(x-3) \cdot 1$$

$$4x - 2(x-3) = x(x-3)$$

$$4x - 2x + 6 = x^2 - 3x$$

$$2x + 6 = x^2 - 3x$$

The result is a quadratic equation. Move everything to one side and then solve for x by factoring the left side and applying the zero-product rule:

$$x^2 - 5x - 6 = 0$$

$$(x + 1)(x - 6) = 0$$

$$x + 1 = 0 \quad \text{or} \quad x - 6 = 0$$

$$x = -1 \qquad\qquad x = 6$$

Therefore, the possible solutions are $x = -1$ and $x = 6$. Since neither of these values will cause division by zero when substituted back into the original equation, they are both valid solutions.

7. C: The score that has approximately 50% above and 50% below is approximately 500 (517 to be exact). The scores can be manually written by choosing either the lower or upper end of each interval and using the frequency to determine the number of times to record each score, i.e., using the lower end of each interval shows an approximate value of 465 for the median; using the upper end of each interval shows an approximate value of 530 for the median. A score of 500 (and the exact median of 517) is found between 465 and 530.

8. C: To divide expressions that contain variables, divide pairs of like variables (or constants) that appear in both the numerator and denominator. For this problem, first divide the constants: $12 \div 3$, then divide the a's: $a^2 \div a$. Since $a^2 \div a$ is equivalent to $\frac{a^2}{a^1}$, use the quotient rule, $\frac{x^a}{x^b} = x^{a-b}$, to simplify it. There is no change to b since the divisor does not contain the variable b :

$$\frac{12a^2b}{3a} = \frac{4a^{2-1}b}{1}$$

$$= 4ab$$

9. C: "The square of twice the sum of x and three is equal to the product of twenty-four and x" is represented by the equation $[2(x + 3)]^2 = 24x$. Solve for x.
$$[2(x + 3)]^2 = 24x$$
$$[2x + 6]^2 = 24x$$
$$4x^2 + 24x + 36 = 24x$$
$$4x^2 = -36$$
$$x^2 = -9$$
$$x = \pm\sqrt{-9}$$
$$x = \pm3i$$

So, $-3i$ is a possible value of x.

10. B: If a line-of-fit is drawn through the points, the slope will be -1/5 so the snow melts 5 centimeters every day.

11. D: The expected value is equal to the sum of the products of each card value and its probability. Thus, the expected value is $\left(1 \cdot \frac{1}{5}\right) + \left(2 \cdot \frac{1}{5}\right) + \left(3 \cdot \frac{1}{5}\right) + \left(4 \cdot \frac{1}{5}\right) + \left(5 \cdot \frac{1}{5}\right)$, which equals 3.

12. B: The number of tails he can expect after 6 coin tosses is equal to the product of the probability of getting tails on one coin toss and the number of coin tosses. Thus, the expected value is $\frac{1}{2} \cdot 6$, or 3.

13. C: In $\triangle ABC$, the midpoints are marked as $D, E,$ and F. The medians of the triangle are then drawn in as $\overline{AF}, \overline{BD}$ and $\overline{CE}$. The medians intersect at a point called the centroid. Based on this intersection, it is the case that $AG = 2GF$, $BG = 2GD$, and $CG = 2GE$. Since we are

given that $BG = 6x - 4$ and $GD = 2x + 8$, we can set up the equation as $6x - 4 = 2(2x + 8)$. Simplifying that equation, it becomes $6x - 4 = 4x + 16$. After subtracting $4x$ from both sides and adding 4 to both sides, the equation becomes $2x = 20$. Divide both sides by 2 to get $x = 10$. Then, the length of $\overline{GD}$ is calculated as $2(10) + 8 = 20 + 8 = 28$.

14. E: First solve for the number of questions Matthew must answer correctly. See the explanation for question 41. To determine the number of correct answers Matthew needs, solve the following inequality:
$$3x > 96$$
$$x > \frac{96}{3}$$
$$x > 32$$
Therefore, Matthew must correctly answer at more than 32 questions to qualify for varsity sports. Since the test has 40 questions, he must answer less than 8 questions incorrectly. Matthew could also answer 0 questions incorrectly. Hence, the best inequality to describe the number of questions Matthew can answer incorrectly is $0 \le x < 8$.

15. C: Use the formula Volume = length x width x height:
$200 = 5 \times 5 \times h$
$25h = 200$

16. B: First, determine how many miles can be driven on one tank of gas by multiplying the numbers of gallons in a tank by the miles per gallon:
12 gallon/tank x 30 miles/gallon = 360 miles
Next, divide the total miles for the trip by the number of miles driven per tank of gas to determine how many total tanks of gas Robert will need:
1,800 miles ÷ 360 miles/tank = 5 tanks

17. B: The slope of a line is a number that represents its steepness. Lines with positive slope go from the bottom-left to the top-right, lines with negative slope go from the top-left to the bottom-right, and horizontal lines have zero slope. You can also think of slope as being $\frac{rise}{run}$. In particular, a slope of 2 (which is equivalent to a slope of 2/1) means that the line rises (goes up) 2 units every time it runs (goes to the right) 1 unit. Looking closely at line k, notice that for every 2 units it goes up, it goes to the right 1 unit.

18. C: The average time can be represented by the expression, $\frac{3}{4}(16) + \frac{1}{4}(12)$, which equals the sum of 12 and 3, or 15. Thus, the average time overall was 15 seconds.

19. B: The events are dependent, since the first marble was not replaced. The sample space of the second draw will decrease by 1 because there will be one less marble to choose. The number of possible red marbles for the second draw will also decrease by 1. Thus, the probability may be written as $P(A \text{ and } B) = \frac{8}{15} \cdot \frac{7}{14}$. The probability he draws a red marble, does not replace it, and draws another red marble is $\frac{4}{15}$.

20. B: Start by squaring both sides of the equation and simplifying the result:

$$\left(\sqrt{3x-2}\right)^2 = (x-2)^2$$
$$3x - 2 = x^2 - 4x + 4$$

Next, move everything to one side and factor to find solutions for x:

$$x^2 - 7x + 6 = 0$$
$$(x - 1)(x - 6) = 0$$
$$x - 1 = 0 \quad \text{or} \quad x - 6 = 0$$
$$x = 1 \qquad\qquad x = 6$$

Therefore, the possible solutions are $x = 1$ and $x = 6$. Substitute these solutions into the original equation to see if they are valid solutions:

$$\sqrt{3x-2} = x - 2 \qquad\qquad \sqrt{3x-2} = x - 2$$
$$\sqrt{3(1)-2} = (1) - 2 \qquad \sqrt{3(6)-2} = (6) - 2$$
$$\sqrt{1} = 1 - 2 \qquad\qquad \sqrt{16} = 6 - 2$$
$$1 = 1 - 2 \ \text{False} \qquad\qquad 4 = 6 - 2 \ \text{True}$$

Since only $x = 6$ leads to a true equality, that is the only solution.

21. E: Get all of the variables on one side of the equation and solve.
$7\sqrt{x} + 16 = 79$
Subtract 16 from both sides of the equation:
$7\sqrt{x} = 63$
Divide both sides by 7:
$\sqrt{x} = 9$
Square both sides:
$x = 81$

22. B: The product given for Choice B can be written as $27x^3 - 9x^2y + 3xy^2 + 9x^2y - 3xy^2 + y^3$, which reduces to $27x^3 + y^3$.

23. D: If $\frac{1}{4}$ inch represents 8 miles, then 1 inch represents 4 x 8 = 32 miles. Two inches represents 2 x 32 = 64 inches. An $\frac{1}{8}$ of a mile represents 8 ÷ 2 = 4 miles. Then $2\frac{1}{8}$ inches represents 64 + 4 = 68 miles.

24. D: To determine the scale factor of the dilation, compare the coordinates of $\triangle J'K'L'$ to the coordinates of $\triangle JKL$. J is at (−2 −3) and J' is at (−4, −6), which means that the coordinates of J were multiplied by a scale factor of 2 to get the coordinates of J'. K is at (1, 3) and K' is at (2, 6). L is at (4, −1) and L' is at (8, −2). As can be seen, the coordinates of K and L were also multiplied by a scale factor of 2 to get to the coordinates of K' and L'.

25. B: The length of an arc is proportional to the measure of the arc, relative to the circle. Here, the length of arc $\widehat{AB}$ is in a ratio of 4:48, or 1:12, with the total circle perimeter. Thus the measure of arc $\widehat{AB}$ has a ratio of 1:12 with the total circle measure, which is always 360°. To find the unknown arc measure, set up a proportion with the known information as follows: $\frac{1}{12} = \frac{x}{360°}$. Solving for x gives $12x = 360°$, or $x = 30°$.

Secret Key #1 - Time is Your Greatest Enemy

Pace Yourself

Wear a watch. At the beginning of the test, check the time (or start a chronometer on your watch to count the minutes), and check the time after every few questions to make sure you are "on schedule."

If you are forced to speed up, do it efficiently. Usually one or more answer choices can be eliminated without too much difficulty. Above all, don't panic. Don't speed up and just begin guessing at random choices. By pacing yourself, and continually monitoring your progress against your watch, you will always know exactly how far ahead or behind you are with your available time. If you find that you are one minute behind on the test, don't skip one question without spending any time on it, just to catch back up. Take 15 fewer seconds on the next four questions, and after four questions you'll have caught back up. Once you catch back up, you can continue working each problem at your normal pace.

Furthermore, don't dwell on the problems that you were rushed on. If a problem was taking up too much time and you made a hurried guess, it must be difficult. The difficult questions are the ones you are most likely to miss anyway, so it isn't a big loss. It is better to end with more time than you need than to run out of time.

Lastly, sometimes it is beneficial to slow down if you are constantly getting ahead of time. You are always more likely to catch a careless mistake by working more slowly than quickly, and among very high-scoring test takers (those who are likely to have lots of time left over), careless errors affect the score more than mastery of material.

Secret Key #2 - Guessing is not Guesswork

You probably know that guessing is a good idea. Unlike other standardized tests, there is no penalty for getting a wrong answer. Even if you have no idea about a question, you still have a 20-25% chance of getting it right.

Most test takers do not understand the impact that proper guessing can have on their score. Unless you score extremely high, guessing will significantly contribute to your final score.

Monkeys Take the Test

What most test takers don't realize is that to insure that 20-25% chance, you have to guess randomly. If you put 20 monkeys in a room to take this test, assuming they answered once per question and behaved themselves, on average they would get 20-25% of the questions correct. Put 20 test takers in the room, and the average will be much lower among guessed questions. Why?
1. The test writers intentionally write deceptive answer choices that "look" right. A test taker has no idea about a question, so he picks the "best looking" answer, which is often wrong. The monkey has no idea what looks good and what doesn't, so it will consistently be right about 20-25% of the time.
2. Test takers will eliminate answer choices from the guessing pool based on a hunch or intuition. Simple but correct answers often get excluded, leaving a 0% chance of being correct. The monkey has no clue, and often gets lucky with the best choice.

This is why the process of elimination endorsed by most test courses is flawed and detrimental to your performance. Test takers don't guess; they make an ignorant stab in the dark that is usually worse than random.

$5 Challenge

Let me introduce one of the most valuable ideas of this course—the $5 challenge:

You only mark your "best guess" if you are willing to bet $5 on it.
You only eliminate choices from guessing if you are willing to bet $5 on it.

Why $5? Five dollars is an amount of money that is small yet not insignificant, and can really add up fast (20 questions could cost you $100). Likewise, each answer choice on one question of the test will have a small impact on your overall score, but it can really add up to a lot of points in the end.

The process of elimination IS valuable. The following shows your chance of guessing it right:

If you eliminate wrong answer choices until only this many remain:	Chance of getting it correct:
1	100%
2	50%
3	33%

However, if you accidentally eliminate the right answer or go on a hunch for an incorrect answer, your chances drop dramatically—to 0%. By guessing among all the answer choices, you are GUARANTEED to have a shot at the right answer.

That's why the $5 test is so valuable. If you give up the advantage and safety of a pure guess, it had better be worth the risk.

What we still haven't covered is how to be sure that whatever guess you make is truly random. Here's the easiest way:

Always pick the first answer choice among those remaining.

Such a technique means that you have decided, **before you see a single test question**, exactly how you are going to guess, and since the order of choices tells you nothing about which one is correct, this guessing technique is perfectly random.

This section is not meant to scare you away from making educated guesses or eliminating choices; you just need to define when a choice is worth eliminating. The $5 test, along with a pre-defined random guessing strategy, is the best way to make sure you reap all of the benefits of guessing.

Secret Key #3 - Practice Smarter, Not Harder

Many test takers delay the test preparation process because they dread the awful amounts of practice time they think necessary to succeed on the test. We have refined an effective method that will take you only a fraction of the time.

There are a number of "obstacles" in the path to success. Among these are answering questions, finishing in time, and mastering test-taking strategies. All must be executed on the day of the test at peak performance, or your score will suffer. The test is a mental marathon that has a large impact on your future.

Just like a marathon runner, it is important to work your way up to the full challenge. So first you just worry about questions, and then time, and finally strategy:

Success Strategy

1. Find a good source for practice tests.
2. If you are willing to make a larger time investment, consider using more than one study guide. Often the different approaches of multiple authors will help you "get" difficult concepts.
3. Take a practice test with no time constraints, with all study helps, "open book." Take your time with questions and focus on applying strategies.
4. Take a practice test with time constraints, with all guides, "open book."
5. Take a final practice test without open material and with time limits.

If you have time to take more practice tests, just repeat step 5. By gradually exposing yourself to the full rigors of the test environment, you will condition your mind to the stress of test day and maximize your success.

Secret Key #4 - Prepare, Don't Procrastinate

Let me state an obvious fact: if you take the test three times, you will probably get three different scores. This is due to the way you feel on test day, the level of preparedness you have, and the version of the test you see. Despite the test writers' claims to the contrary, some versions of the test WILL be easier for you than others.

Since your future depends so much on your score, you should maximize your chances of success. In order to maximize the likelihood of success, you've got to prepare in advance. This means taking practice tests and spending time learning the information and test taking strategies you will need to succeed.

Never go take the actual test as a "practice" test, expecting that you can just take it again if you need to. Take all the practice tests you can on your own, but when you go to take the official test, be prepared, be focused, and do your best the first time!

Secret Key #5 - Test Yourself

Everyone knows that time is money. There is no need to spend too much of your time or too little of your time preparing for the test. You should only spend as much of your precious time preparing as is necessary for you to get the score you need.

Once you have taken a practice test under real conditions of time constraints, then you will know if you are ready for the test or not.

If you have scored extremely high the first time that you take the practice test, then there is not much point in spending countless hours studying. You are already there.

Benchmark your abilities by retaking practice tests and seeing how much you have improved. Once you consistently score high enough to guarantee success, then you are ready.

If you have scored well below where you need, then knuckle down and begin studying in earnest. Check your improvement regularly through the use of practice tests under real conditions. Above all, don't worry, panic, or give up. The key is perseverance!

Then, when you go to take the test, remain confident and remember how well you did on the practice tests. If you can score high enough on a practice test, then you can do the same on the real thing.

General Strategies

The most important thing you can do is to ignore your fears and jump into the test immediately- do not be overwhelmed by any strange-sounding terms. You have to jump into the test like jumping into a pool- all at once is the easiest way.

Make Predictions

As you read and understand the question, try to guess what the answer will be. Remember that several of the answer choices are wrong, and once you begin reading them, your mind will immediately become cluttered with answer choices designed to throw you off. Your mind is typically the most focused immediately after you have read the question and digested its contents. If you can, try to predict what the correct answer will be. You may be surprised at what you can predict.

Quickly scan the choices and see if your prediction is in the listed answer choices. If it is, then you can be quite confident that you have the right answer. It still won't hurt to check the other answer choices, but most of the time, you've got it!

Answer the Question

It may seem obvious to only pick answer choices that answer the question, but the test writers can create some excellent answer choices that are wrong. Don't pick an answer just because it sounds right, or you believe it to be true. It MUST answer the question. Once you've made your selection, always go back and check it against the question and make sure that you didn't misread the question, and the answer choice does answer the question posed.

Benchmark

After you read the first answer choice, decide if you think it sounds correct or not. If it doesn't, move on to the next answer choice. If it does, mentally mark that answer choice. This doesn't mean that you've definitely selected it as your answer choice, it just means that it's the best you've seen thus far. Go ahead and read the next choice. If the next choice is worse than the one you've already selected, keep going to the next answer choice. If the next choice is better than the choice you've already selected, mentally mark the new answer choice as your best guess.

The first answer choice that you select becomes your standard. Every other answer choice must be benchmarked against that standard. That choice is correct until proven otherwise by another answer choice beating it out. Once you've decided that no other answer choice seems as good, do one final check to ensure that your answer choice answers the question posed.

Valid Information

Don't discount any of the information provided in the question. Every piece of information may be necessary to determine the correct answer. None of the information in the question is there to throw you off (while the answer choices will certainly have information to throw you off). If two seemingly unrelated topics are discussed, don't ignore either. You can be confident there is a relationship, or it wouldn't be included in the question, and you are probably going to have to determine what is that relationship to find the answer.

Avoid "Fact Traps"

Don't get distracted by a choice that is factually true. Your search is for the answer that answers the question. Stay focused and don't fall for an answer that is true but incorrect. Always go back to the question and make sure you're choosing an answer that actually answers the question and is not just a true statement. An answer can be factually correct, but it MUST answer the question asked. Additionally, two answers can both be seemingly correct, so be sure to read all of the answer choices, and make sure that you get the one that BEST answers the question.

Milk the Question

Some of the questions may throw you completely off. They might deal with a subject you have not been exposed to, or one that you haven't reviewed in years. While your lack of knowledge about the subject will be a hindrance, the question itself can give you many clues that will help you find the correct answer. Read the question carefully and look for clues. Watch particularly for adjectives and nouns describing difficult terms or words that you don't recognize. Regardless of if you completely understand a word or not, replacing it with a synonym either provided or one you more familiar with may help you to understand what the questions are asking. Rather than wracking your mind about specific detailed information concerning a difficult term or word, try to use mental substitutes that are easier to understand.

The Trap of Familiarity

Don't just choose a word because you recognize it. On difficult questions, you may not recognize a number of words in the answer choices. The test writers don't put "make-believe" words on the test; so don't think that just because you only recognize all the words in one answer choice means that answer choice must be correct. If you only recognize words in one answer choice, then focus on that one. Is it correct? Try your best to determine if it is correct. If it is, that is great, but if it doesn't, eliminate it. Each word and answer choice you eliminate increases your chances of getting the question correct, even if you then have to guess among the unfamiliar choices.

Eliminate Answers

Eliminate choices as soon as you realize they are wrong. But be careful! Make sure you consider all of the possible answer choices. Just because one appears right, doesn't mean that the next one won't be even better! The test writers will usually put more than one good answer choice for every question, so read all of them. Don't worry if you are stuck between two that seem right. By getting down to just two remaining possible choices, your odds are now 50/50. Rather than wasting too much time, play the odds. You are guessing, but guessing wisely, because you've been able to knock out some of the answer choices that you know are wrong. If you are eliminating choices and realize that the last answer choice you are left with is also obviously wrong, don't panic. Start over and consider each choice again. There may easily be something that you missed the first time and will realize on the second pass.

Tough Questions

If you are stumped on a problem or it appears too hard or too difficult, don't waste time. Move on! Remember though, if you can quickly check for obviously incorrect answer choices, your chances of guessing correctly are greatly improved. Before you completely give up, at least try to knock out a couple of possible answers. Eliminate what you can and then guess at the remaining answer choices before moving on.

Brainstorm

If you get stuck on a difficult question, spend a few seconds quickly brainstorming. Run through the complete list of possible answer choices. Look at each choice and ask yourself, "Could this answer the question satisfactorily?" Go through each answer choice and consider it independently of the other. By systematically going through all possibilities, you may find something that you would otherwise overlook. Remember that when you get stuck, it's important to try to keep moving.

Read Carefully

Understand the problem. Read the question and answer choices carefully. Don't miss the question because you misread the terms. You have plenty of time to read each question thoroughly and make sure you understand what is being asked. Yet a happy medium must be attained, so don't waste too much time. You must read carefully, but efficiently.

Face Value

When in doubt, use common sense. Always accept the situation in the problem at face value. Don't read too much into it. These problems will not require you to make huge leaps of logic. The test writers aren't trying to throw you off with a cheap trick. If you have to go beyond creativity and make a leap of logic in order to have an answer choice answer the question, then you should look at the other answer choices. Don't overcomplicate the problem by creating theoretical relationships or explanations that will warp time or space. These are normal problems rooted in reality. It's just that the applicable relationship or explanation may not be readily apparent and you have to figure things out. Use your common sense to interpret anything that isn't clear.

Prefixes

If you're having trouble with a word in the question or answer choices, try dissecting it. Take advantage of every clue that the word might include. Prefixes and suffixes can be a huge help. Usually they allow you to determine a basic meaning. Pre- means before, post- means after, pro - is positive, de- is negative. From these prefixes and suffixes, you can get an idea of the general meaning of the word and try to put it into context. Beware though of any traps. Just because con is the opposite of pro, doesn't necessarily mean congress is the opposite of progress!

Hedge Phrases

Watch out for critical "hedge" phrases, such as likely, may, can, will often, sometimes, often, almost, mostly, usually, generally, rarely, sometimes. Question writers insert these hedge phrases to cover every possibility. Often an answer choice will be wrong simply because it leaves no room for exception. Avoid answer choices that have definitive words like "exactly," and "always".

Switchback Words

Stay alert for "switchbacks". These are the words and phrases frequently used to alert you to shifts in thought. The most common switchback word is "but". Others include although, however, nevertheless, on the other hand, even though, while, in spite of, despite, regardless of.

New Information

Correct answer choices will rarely have completely new information included. Answer choices typically are straightforward reflections of the material asked about and will directly relate to the question. If a new piece of information is included in an answer choice that doesn't even seem to relate to the topic being asked about, then that answer choice is likely incorrect. All of the information needed to answer the question is usually provided for you, and so you should not have to make guesses that are unsupported or choose answer choices that require unknown information that cannot be reasoned on its own.

Time Management

On technical questions, don't get lost on the technical terms. Don't spend too much time on any one question. If you don't know what a term means, then since you don't have a dictionary, odds are you aren't going to get much further. You should immediately recognize terms as whether or not you know them. If you don't, work with the other clues that you have, the other answer choices and terms provided, but don't waste too much time trying to figure out a difficult term.

Contextual Clues

Look for contextual clues. An answer can be right but not correct. The contextual clues will help you find the answer that is most right and is correct. Understand the context in which a phrase or statement is made. This will help you make important distinctions.

Don't Panic

Panicking will not answer any questions for you. Therefore, it isn't helpful. When you first see the question, if your mind goes blank, take a deep breath. Force yourself to mechanically go through the steps of solving the problem and using the strategies you've learned.

Pace Yourself

Don't get clock fever. It's easy to be overwhelmed when you're looking at a page full of questions, your mind is full of random thoughts and feeling confused, and the clock is ticking down faster than you would like. Calm down and maintain the pace that you have set for yourself. As long as you are on track by monitoring your pace, you are guaranteed to have enough time for yourself. When you get to the last few minutes of the test, it may seem like you won't have enough time left, but if you only have as many questions as you should have left at that point, then you're right on track!

Answer Selection

The best way to pick an answer choice is to eliminate all of those that are wrong, until only one is left and confirm that is the correct answer. Sometimes though, an answer choice may immediately look right. Be careful! Take a second to make sure that the other choices are not equally obvious. Don't make a hasty mistake. There are only two times that you should stop before checking other answers. First is when you are positive that the answer choice you have selected is correct. Second is when time is almost out and you have to make a quick guess!

Check Your Work

Since you will probably not know every term listed and the answer to every question, it is important that you get credit for the ones that you do know. Don't miss any questions through careless mistakes. If at all possible, try to take a second to look back over your answer selection and make sure you've selected the correct answer choice and haven't made a costly careless mistake (such as marking an answer choice that you didn't mean to mark). This quick double check should more than pay for itself in caught mistakes for the time it costs.

Beware of Directly Quoted Answers

Sometimes an answer choice will repeat word for word a portion of the question or reference section. However, beware of such exact duplication – it may be a trap! More than likely, the correct choice will paraphrase or summarize a point, rather than being exactly the same wording.

Slang

Scientific sounding answers are better than slang ones. An answer choice that begins "To compare the outcomes..." is much more likely to be correct than one that begins "Because some people insisted..."

Extreme Statements

Avoid wild answers that throw out highly controversial ideas that are proclaimed as established fact. An answer choice that states the "process should be used in certain situations, if..." is much more likely to be correct than one that states the "process should be discontinued completely." The first is a calm rational statement and doesn't even make a definitive, uncompromising stance, using a hedge word "if" to provide wiggle room, whereas the second choice is a radical idea and far more extreme.

Answer Choice Families

When you have two or more answer choices that are direct opposites or parallels, one of them is usually the correct answer. For instance, if one answer choice states "x increases" and another answer choice states "x decreases" or "y increases," then those two or three answer choices are very similar in construction and fall into the same family of answer choices. A family of answer choices is when two or three answer choices are very similar in construction, and yet often have a directly opposite meaning. Usually the correct answer choice will be in that family of answer choices. The "odd man out" or answer choice that doesn't seem to fit the parallel construction of the other answer choices is more likely to be incorrect.

Special Report: How to Overcome Test Anxiety

The very nature of tests caters to some level of anxiety, nervousness, or tension, just as we feel for any important event that occurs in our lives. A little bit of anxiety or nervousness can be a good thing. It helps us with motivation, and makes achievement just that much sweeter. However, too much anxiety can be a problem, especially if it hinders our ability to function and perform.

"Test anxiety," is the term that refers to the emotional reactions that some test-takers experience when faced with a test or exam. Having a fear of testing and exams is based upon a rational fear, since the test-taker's performance can shape the course of an academic career. Nevertheless, experiencing excessive fear of examinations will only interfere with the test-taker's ability to perform and chance to be successful.

There are a large variety of causes that can contribute to the development and sensation of test anxiety. These include, but are not limited to, lack of preparation and worrying about issues surrounding the test.

Lack of Preparation

Lack of preparation can be identified by the following behaviors or situations:

- Not scheduling enough time to study, and therefore cramming the night before the test or exam
- Managing time poorly, to create the sensation that there is not enough time to do everything
- Failing to organize the text information in advance, so that the study material consists of the entire text and not simply the pertinent information
- Poor overall studying habits

Worrying, on the other hand, can be related to both the test taker, or many other factors around him/her that will be affected by the results of the test. These include worrying about:

- Previous performances on similar exams, or exams in general
- How friends and other students are achieving
- The negative consequences that will result from a poor grade or failure

There are three primary elements to test anxiety. Physical components, which involve the same typical bodily reactions as those to acute anxiety (to be discussed below). Emotional factors have to do with fear or panic. Mental or cognitive issues concerning attention spans and memory abilities.

Physical Signals

There are many different symptoms of test anxiety, and these are not limited to mental and emotional strain. Frequently there are a range of physical signals that will let a test taker know that he/she is suffering from test anxiety. These bodily changes can include the following:

- Perspiring
- Sweaty palms
- Wet, trembling hands
- Nausea
- Dry mouth
- A knot in the stomach
- Headache
- Faintness
- Muscle tension
- Aching shoulders, back and neck
- Rapid heart beat
- Feeling too hot/cold

To recognize the sensation of test anxiety, a test-taker should monitor him/herself for the following sensations:

- The physical distress symptoms as listed above
- Emotional sensitivity, expressing emotional feelings such as the need to cry or laugh too much, or a sensation of anger or helplessness
- A decreased ability to think, causing the test-taker to blank out or have racing thoughts that are hard to organize or control.

Though most students will feel some level of anxiety when faced with a test or exam, the majority can cope with that anxiety and maintain it at a manageable level. However, those who cannot are faced with a very real and very serious condition, which can and should be controlled for the immeasurable benefit of this sufferer.

Naturally, these sensations lead to negative results for the testing experience. The most common effects of test anxiety have to do with nervousness and mental blocking.

Nervousness

Nervousness can appear in several different levels:

- The test-taker's difficulty, or even inability to read and understand the questions on the test
- The difficulty or inability to organize thoughts to a coherent form
- The difficulty or inability to recall key words and concepts relating to the testing questions (especially essays)
- The receipt of poor grades on a test, though the test material was well known by the test taker

Conversely, a person may also experience mental blocking, which involves:

- Blanking out on test questions
- Only remembering the correct answers to the questions when the test has already finished.

Fortunately for test anxiety sufferers, beating these feelings, to a large degree, has to do with proper preparation. When a test taker has a feeling of preparedness, then anxiety will be dramatically lessened.

The first step to resolving anxiety issues is to distinguish which of the two types of anxiety are being suffered. If the anxiety is a direct result of a lack of preparation, this should be considered a normal reaction, and the anxiety level (as opposed to the test results) shouldn't be anything to worry about. However, if, when adequately prepared, the test-taker still panics, blanks out, or seems to overreact, this is not a fully rational reaction. While this can be considered normal too, there are many ways to combat and overcome these effects.

Remember that anxiety cannot be entirely eliminated, however, there are ways to minimize it, to make the anxiety easier to manage. Preparation is one of the best ways to minimize test anxiety. Therefore the following techniques are wise in order to best fight off any anxiety that may want to build.

To begin with, try to avoid cramming before a test, whenever it is possible. By trying to memorize an entire term's worth of information in one day, you'll be shocking your system, and not giving yourself a very good chance to absorb the information. This is an easy path to anxiety, so for those who suffer from test anxiety, cramming should not even be considered an option.

Instead of cramming, work throughout the semester to combine all of the material which is presented throughout the semester, and work on it gradually as the course goes by, making sure to master the main concepts first, leaving minor details for a week or so before the test.

To study for the upcoming exam, be sure to pose questions that may be on the examination, to gauge the ability to answer them by integrating the ideas from your texts, notes and lectures, as well as any supplementary readings.

If it is truly impossible to cover all of the information that was covered in that particular term, concentrate on the most important portions, that can be covered very well. Learn these concepts as best as possible, so that when the test comes, a goal can be made to use these concepts as presentations of your knowledge.

In addition to study habits, changes in attitude are critical to beating a struggle with test anxiety. In fact, an improvement of the perspective over the entire test-taking experience can actually help a test taker to enjoy studying and therefore improve the overall experience. Be certain not to overemphasize the significance of the grade - know that the result of the test is neither a reflection of self worth, nor is it a measure of intelligence; one grade will not predict a person's future success.

To improve an overall testing outlook, the following steps should be tried:
- Keeping in mind that the most reasonable expectation for taking a test is to expect to try to demonstrate as much of what you know as you possibly can.
- Reminding ourselves that a test is only one test; this is not the only one, and there will be others.
- The thought of thinking of oneself in an irrational, all-or-nothing term should be avoided at all costs.
- A reward should be designated for after the test, so there's something to look forward to. Whether it be going to a movie, going out to eat, or simply visiting friends, schedule it in advance, and do it no matter what result is expected on the exam.

Test-takers should also keep in mind that the basics are some of the most important things, even beyond anti-anxiety techniques and studying. Never neglect the basic social, emotional and biological needs, in order to try to absorb information. In order to best achieve, these three factors must be held as just as important as the studying itself.

Study Steps

Remember the following important steps for studying:

- Maintain healthy nutrition and exercise habits. Continue both your recreational activities and social pass times. These both contribute to your physical and emotional well being.
- Be certain to get a good amount of sleep, especially the night before the test, because when you're overtired you are not able to perform to the best of your best ability.
- Keep the studying pace to a moderate level by taking breaks when they are needed, and varying the work whenever possible, to keep the mind fresh instead of getting bored.
- When enough studying has been done that all the material that can be learned has been learned, and the test taker is prepared for the test, stop studying and do something relaxing such as listening to music, watching a movie, or taking a warm bubble bath.

There are also many other techniques to minimize the uneasiness or apprehension that is experienced along with test anxiety before, during, or even after the examination. In fact, there are a great deal of things that can be done to stop anxiety from interfering with lifestyle and performance. Again, remember that anxiety will not be eliminated entirely, and it shouldn't be. Otherwise that "up" feeling for exams would not exist, and most of us depend on that sensation to perform better than usual. However, this anxiety has to be at a level that is manageable.

Of course, as we have just discussed, being prepared for the exam is half the battle right away. Attending all classes, finding out what knowledge will be expected on the exam, and knowing the exam schedules are easy steps to lowering anxiety. Keeping up with work will remove the need to cram, and efficient study habits will eliminate wasted time. Studying should be done in an ideal location for concentration, so that it is simple to become interested in the material and give it complete attention. A method such as SQ3R (Survey,

Question, Read, Recite, Review) is a wonderful key to follow to make sure that the study habits are as effective as possible, especially in the case of learning from a textbook. Flashcards are great techniques for memorization. Learning to take good notes will mean that notes will be full of useful information, so that less sifting will need to be done to seek out what is pertinent for studying. Reviewing notes after class and then again on occasion will keep the information fresh in the mind. From notes that have been taken summary sheets and outlines can be made for simpler reviewing.

A study group can also be a very motivational and helpful place to study, as there will be a sharing of ideas, all of the minds can work together, to make sure that everyone understands, and the studying will be made more interesting because it will be a social occasion. Basically, though, as long as the test-taker remains organized and self confident, with efficient study habits, less time will need to be spent studying, and higher grades will be achieved.

To become self confident, there are many useful steps. The first of these is "self talk." It has been shown through extensive research, that self-talk for students who suffer from test anxiety, should be well monitored, in order to make sure that it contributes to self confidence as opposed to sinking the student. Frequently the self talk of test-anxious students is negative or self-defeating, thinking that everyone else is smarter and faster, that they always mess up, and that if they don't do well, they'll fail the entire course. It is important to decreasing anxiety that awareness is made of self talk. Try writing any negative self thoughts and then disputing them with a positive statement instead. Begin self-encouragement as though it was a friend speaking. Repeat positive statements to help reprogram the mind to believing in successes instead of failures.

Helpful Techniques

Other extremely helpful techniques include:

- Self-visualization of doing well and reaching goals
- While aiming for an "A" level of understanding, don't try to "overprotect" by setting your expectations lower. This will only convince the mind to stop studying in order to meet the lower expectations.
- Don't make comparisons with the results or habits of other students. These are individual factors, and different things work for different people, causing different results.
- Strive to become an expert in learning what works well, and what can be done in order to improve. Consider collecting this data in a journal.
- Create rewards for after studying instead of doing things before studying that will only turn into avoidance behaviors.
- Make a practice of relaxing - by using methods such as progressive relaxation, self-hypnosis, guided imagery, etc - in order to make relaxation an automatic sensation.
- Work on creating a state of relaxed concentration so that concentrating will take on the focus of the mind, so that none will be wasted on worrying.
- Take good care of the physical self by eating well and getting enough sleep.
- Plan in time for exercise and stick to this plan.

Beyond these techniques, there are other methods to be used before, during and after the test that will help the test-taker perform well in addition to overcoming anxiety.

Before the exam comes the academic preparation. This involves establishing a study schedule and beginning at least one week before the actual date of the test. By doing this, the anxiety of not having enough time to study for the test will be automatically eliminated. Moreover, this will make the studying a much more effective experience, ensuring that the learning will be an easier process. This relieves much undue pressure on the test-taker.

Summary sheets, note cards, and flash cards with the main concepts and examples of these main concepts should be prepared in advance of the actual studying time. A topic should never be eliminated from this process. By omitting a topic because it isn't expected to be on the test is only setting up the test-taker for anxiety should it actually appear on the exam. Utilize the course syllabus for laying out the topics that should be studied. Carefully go over the notes that were made in class, paying special attention to any of the issues that the professor took special care to emphasize while lecturing in class. In the textbooks, use the chapter review, or if possible, the chapter tests, to begin your review.

It may even be possible to ask the instructor what information will be covered on the exam, or what the format of the exam will be (for example, multiple choice, essay, free form, true-false). Additionally, see if it is possible to find out how many questions will be on the test. If a review sheet or sample test has been offered by the professor, make good use of it, above anything else, for the preparation for the test. Another great resource for getting to know the examination is reviewing tests from previous semesters. Use these tests to review, and aim to achieve a 100% score on each of the possible topics. With a few exceptions, the goal that you set for yourself is the highest one that you will reach.

Take all of the questions that were assigned as homework, and rework them to any other possible course material. The more problems reworked, the more skill and confidence will form as a result. When forming the solution to a problem, write out each of the steps. Don't simply do head work. By doing as many steps on paper as possible, much clarification and therefore confidence will be formed. Do this with as many homework problems as possible, before checking the answers. By checking the answer after each problem, a reinforcement will exist, that will not be on the exam. Study situations should be as exam-like as possible, to prime the test-taker's system for the experience. By waiting to check the answers at the end, a psychological advantage will be formed, to decrease the stress factor.

Another fantastic reason for not cramming is the avoidance of confusion in concepts, especially when it comes to mathematics. 8-10 hours of study will become one hundred percent more effective if it is spread out over a week or at least several days, instead of doing it all in one sitting. Recognize that the human brain requires time in order to assimilate new material, so frequent breaks and a span of study time over several days will be much more beneficial.

Additionally, don't study right up until the point of the exam. Studying should stop a minimum of one hour before the exam begins. This allows the brain to rest and put things in their proper order. This will also provide the time to become as relaxed as possible when going into the examination room. The test-taker will also have time to eat well and eat sensibly. Know that the brain needs food as much as the rest of the body. With enough food and enough sleep, as well as a relaxed attitude, the body and the mind are primed for success.

Avoid any anxious classmates who are talking about the exam. These students only spread anxiety, and are not worth sharing the anxious sentimentalities.

Before the test also involves creating a positive attitude, so mental preparation should also be a point of concentration. There are many keys to creating a positive attitude. Should fears become rushing in, make a visualization of taking the exam, doing well, and seeing an A written on the paper. Write out a list of affirmations that will bring a feeling of confidence, such as "I am doing well in my English class," "I studied well and know my material," "I enjoy this class." Even if the affirmations aren't believed at first, it sends a positive message to the subconscious which will result in an alteration of the overall belief system, which is the system that creates reality.

If a sensation of panic begins, work with the fear and imagine the very worst! Work through the entire scenario of not passing the test, failing the entire course, and dropping out of school, followed by not getting a job, and pushing a shopping cart through the dark alley where you'll live. This will place things into perspective! Then, practice deep breathing and create a visualization of the opposite situation - achieving an "A" on the exam, passing the entire course, receiving the degree at a graduation ceremony.

On the day of the test, there are many things to be done to ensure the best results, as well as the most calm outlook. The following stages are suggested in order to maximize test-taking potential:

- Begin the examination day with a moderate breakfast, and avoid any coffee or beverages with caffeine if the test taker is prone to jitters. Even people who are used to managing caffeine can feel jittery or light-headed when it is taken on a test day.
- Attempt to do something that is relaxing before the examination begins. As last minute cramming clouds the mastering of overall concepts, it is better to use this time to create a calming outlook.
- Be certain to arrive at the test location well in advance, in order to provide time to select a location that is away from doors, windows and other distractions, as well as giving enough time to relax before the test begins.
- Keep away from anxiety generating classmates who will upset the sensation of stability and relaxation that is being attempted before the exam.
- Should the waiting period before the exam begins cause anxiety, create a self-distraction by reading a light magazine or something else that is relaxing and simple.

During the exam itself, read the entire exam from beginning to end, and find out how much time should be allotted to each individual problem. Once writing the exam, should more time be taken for a problem, it should be abandoned, in order to begin another problem. If there is time at the end, the unfinished problem can always be returned to and completed.

Read the instructions very carefully - twice - so that unpleasant surprises won't follow during or after the exam has ended.

When writing the exam, pretend that the situation is actually simply the completion of homework within a library, or at home. This will assist in forming a relaxed atmosphere, and will allow the brain extra focus for the complex thinking function.

Begin the exam with all of the questions with which the most confidence is felt. This will build the confidence level regarding the entire exam and will begin a quality momentum. This will also create encouragement for trying the problems where uncertainty resides.

Going with the "gut instinct" is always the way to go when solving a problem. Second guessing should be avoided at all costs. Have confidence in the ability to do well.

For essay questions, create an outline in advance that will keep the mind organized and make certain that all of the points are remembered. For multiple choice, read every answer, even if the correct one has been spotted - a better one may exist.

Continue at a pace that is reasonable and not rushed, in order to be able to work carefully. Provide enough time to go over the answers at the end, to check for small errors that can be corrected.

Should a feeling of panic begin, breathe deeply, and think of the feeling of the body releasing sand through its pores. Visualize a calm, peaceful place, and include all of the sights, sounds and sensations of this image. Continue the deep breathing, and take a few minutes to continue this with closed eyes. When all is well again, return to the test.

If a "blanking" occurs for a certain question, skip it and move on to the next question. There will be time to return to the other question later. Get everything done that can be done, first, to guarantee all the grades that can be compiled, and to build all of the confidence possible. Then return to the weaker questions to build the marks from there.

Remember, one's own reality can be created, so as long as the belief is there, success will follow. And remember: anxiety can happen later, right now, there's an exam to be written!

After the examination is complete, whether there is a feeling for a good grade or a bad grade, don't dwell on the exam, and be certain to follow through on the reward that was promised...and enjoy it! Don't dwell on any mistakes that have been made, as there is nothing that can be done at this point anyway.

Additionally, don't begin to study for the next test right away. Do something relaxing for a while, and let the mind relax and prepare itself to begin absorbing information again.

From the results of the exam - both the grade and the entire experience, be certain to learn from what has gone on. Perfect studying habits and work some more on confidence in order to make the next examination experience even better than the last one.

Learn to avoid places where openings occurred for laziness, procrastination and day dreaming.

Use the time between this exam and the next one to better learn to relax, even learning to relax on cue, so that any anxiety can be controlled during the next exam. Learn how to relax the body. Slouch in your chair if that helps. Tighten and then relax all of the different muscle groups, one group at a time, beginning with the feet and then working all the way up to the neck and face. This will ultimately relax the muscles more than they were to begin with. Learn how to breathe deeply and comfortably, and focus on this breathing going in and out as a relaxing thought. With every exhale, repeat the word "relax."

As common as test anxiety is, it is very possible to overcome it. Make yourself one of the test-takers who overcome this frustrating hindrance.

Special Report: Retaking the Test: What Are Your Chances at Improving Your Score?

After going through the experience of taking a major test, many test takers feel that once is enough. The test usually comes during a period of transition in the test taker's life, and taking the test is only one of a series of important events. With so many distractions and conflicting recommendations, it may be difficult for a test taker to rationally determine whether or not he should retake the test after viewing his scores.

The importance of the test usually only adds to the burden of the retake decision. However, don't be swayed by emotion. There a few simple questions that you can ask yourself to guide you as you try to determine whether a retake would improve your score:

1. What went wrong? Why wasn't your score what you expected?

Can you point to a single factor or problem that you feel caused the low score? Were you sick on test day? Was there an emotional upheaval in your life that caused a distraction? Were you late for the test or not able to use the full time allotment? If you can point to any of these specific, individual problems, then a retake should definitely be considered.

2. Is there enough time to improve?

Many problems that may show up in your score report may take a lot of time for improvement. A deficiency in a particular math skill may require weeks or months of tutoring and studying to improve. If you have enough time to improve an identified weakness, then a retake should definitely be considered.

3. How will additional scores be used? Will a score average, highest score, or most recent score be used?

Different test scores may be handled completely differently. If you've taken the test multiple times, sometimes your highest score is used, sometimes your average score is computed and used, and sometimes your most recent score is used. Make sure you understand what method will be used to evaluate your scores, and use that to help you determine whether a retake should be considered.

4. Are my practice test scores significantly higher than my actual test score?

If you have taken a lot of practice tests and are consistently scoring at a much higher level than your actual test score, then you should consider a retake. However, if you've taken five practice tests and only one of your scores was higher than your actual test score, or if your practice test scores were only slightly higher than your actual test score, then it is unlikely that you will significantly increase your score.

5. Do I need perfect scores or will I be able to live with this score? Will this score still allow me to follow my dreams?

What kind of score is acceptable to you? Is your current score "good enough?" Do you have to have a certain score in order to pursue the future of your dreams? If you won't be happy with your current score, and there's no way that you could live with it, then you should consider a retake. However, don't get your hopes up. If you are looking for significant improvement, that may or may not be possible. But if you won't be happy otherwise, it is at least worth the effort.
Remember that there are other considerations. To achieve your dream, it is likely that your grades may also be taken into account. A great test score is usually not the only thing necessary to succeed. Make sure that you aren't overemphasizing the importance of a high test score.

Furthermore, a retake does not always result in a higher score. Some test takers will score lower on a retake, rather than higher. One study shows that one-fourth of test takers will achieve a significant improvement in test score, while one-sixth of test takers will actually show a decrease. While this shows that most test takers will improve, the majority will only improve their scores a little and a retake may not be worth the test taker's effort.

Finally, if a test is taken only once and is considered in the added context of good grades on the part of a test taker, the person reviewing the grades and scores may be tempted to assume that the test taker just had a bad day while taking the test, and may discount the low test score in favor of the high grades. But if the test is retaken and the scores are approximately the same, then the validity of the low scores are only confirmed. Therefore, a retake could actually hurt a test taker by definitely bracketing a test taker's score ability to a limited range.

Additional Bonus Material

Due to our efforts to try to keep this book to a manageable length, we've created a link that will give you access to all of your additional bonus material.

Please visit http://www.mometrix.com/bonus948/ssatupper to access the information.